Breakthrough Partnering

Oliver Wight Publications, Inc.

EXECUTIVE BREAKTHROUGH SERIES

Breakthrough Partnering: Creating a
Collective Enterprise Advantage
by Patricia E. Moody

In the Age of the Real-Time Enterprise
by Tom Gunn (Available March 1994)

Planning & Control in the Age of Lean Production
by Darryl V. Landvater (Available February 1994)

Quantum Leap: Achieving Strategic
Breakthroughs with QFD
by Thomas F. Wallace and William Barnard
(Available January 1994)

Recreating the Workplace: The Pathway
to High Performance Work Systems,
by Steven R. Rayner

Reengineering: Leveraging the Power of
Integrated Product Development
by V. Daniel Hunt

Breakthrough Partnering

**CREATING A COLLECTIVE
ENTERPRISE ADVANTAGE**

Patricia E. Moody

omneo

An imprint of
Oliver Wight Publications, Inc.
85 Allen Martin Drive
Essex Junction, VT 05452

For Delia Richard Moody
1917–1972
who drilled me in Dick and Jane until
the letters made words.

Acknowledgments

Believers, supporters, critics, and practitioners—all have contributed to this work. Writing a book is hard labor; I appreciate my family's patience because they understood how difficult and important it was to write. Two unnamed executives who modeled traditional purchasing practice provided much negative energy—surely this could be done better! Fortunately, U.S. industry is also populated with executives who share sometimes opposing but complementary talents—an ability to get things done in today's world and great understanding of tomorrow's possibilities. They are the ones I need to recognize for helping to form the vision of Breakthrough Partnering:

Dave Nelson, Vice President of Purchasing, Honda of America

Mike Schoonover, Vice President of Operations, EMC Corporation

The Association for Manufacturing Excellence Customer Supplier Partnership Team (CUSSUPS): Robert W. Hall, Ken Stork, Bob Useller (McNeil), Ralph Todd, Dave Curry (Honda of America), Bob Fulford (Varian Research Associates), Jim Schwarz (President, OMNI-Circuits)

Bob LeValley ("Dr. Bob"), Solectron

Donna Neusch and Alan Siebenaler, who "finished" first

Deborah Kolb, Harvard University

Jeff Anderson, Williams Technologies

Kevin Wade, Honda of America, for his benchmarking input

Richard Cole, Chairman, Lytron

Bonnie Klane, Director of Human Resource Management, EMC Corporation

Paul Jenson, Nypro Institute

Paul Brault, Motorola

Contents

Contents

List of Figures and Tables

FIGURES

TABLES

Introduction

My first job was purchasing. I lived with a ten-ton Frieden calculator on my desk and a two-line phone attached to my ear. Every morning another twenty to twenty-five purchase orders appeared, followed by an equal number of shipping documents to match and pay. Although our department spent millions yearly, we never set foot in the factory, and only about twice a year did we venture into our vendor's shop. It was a paper world, completely isolated from customers and suppliers.

Naturally, the next stop for me was manufacturing, "the heart of the beast." Steel mills, pharmaceuticals, aircraft parts and assemblies, machine shops (my favorite), printing plants, paper mills, metal bangers, textiles, printed circuit boards, machine tools, the whole exciting range of noisy, busy places where people make things.

Manufacturing is addictive. It grew on me from the first time my father lifted me up to look down into a vat of pulp, one day away from construction paper. We lived across from the Nissitissit River in Pepperell, Massachusetts, a mill town that two hundred years before had supported a gristmill and a lumbermill. Everyone in town had at one time or another worked in one of the three remaining factories: St. Regis Paper Company, Bemis Bag, and the Pepperell Braiding Factory. The factory whistles signaled lunchtime for the whole town: Dads came home for lunch and kids unwrapped the sandwiches they had carried to school in Bemis sugar bags. You grew up with an awareness of how important the factory was to your town's daily existence. When the end came and most of the machinery moved down South, the town became a shell.

I remember running into the house through my mother's freshly hung out clothes to ask, "What was the big bang?" The old penstock, a conduit for conveying water to a waterwheel and, later, to a steam power plant that ran along the Nashua River papermill's power plant had blown up—we'd heard the explosions two miles upriver.

Now, the stand-alone massively integrated manufacturing concept has reached its limit, and the old water-powered clusters of shops have had their day. Almost two hundred years after Francis Cabot Lowell captured the imagination of a group of investors with the possibilities of integrating in one spot all the previously farmed-out stages of textile manufacture, the manufacturing world is undergoing another massive shift. In 1814, "leading edge" meant factory design, the production layout and mechanical engineering necessary to develop economies of scale—the gears and overhead leather belts of the early industrial age.

In the nineties, the "leading edge" is about people, systems, and communications. Manufacturing is at another turning point, quieter than the exploding penstock, but equally dynamic. Companies that grew by successfully building bigger operations must now think small and light; they must remake themselves by reaching outside their own walls to find suitable teammates. The result will be what I call *enterprise teams*. The goal of the enterprise teams is still to win, but the rules and the playing field have changed. Traditional practices and values, such as company loyalty, leveraged power, and pen-and-paper agreements, are all up for reexamination.

When new organizations and enterprises form, new leaders appear. This book is designed to help the innovators become leaders in the new manufacturing enterprise. The stories and step-by-step guides to the process are tools offered to help leaders see the vision and exercise their communications skills. After all, 90 percent of the work of building these new enterprises is communications, and the ability to communicate, like most things, only gets better with practice.

Breakthrough
Partnering

CHAPTER 1

The Vision: Creating a Collective Enterprise Advantage

When J. Ignacio Lopez de Arriortua, General Motors' former head of purchasing, arrived in Detroit from Europe in 1992, he mandated a "new" approach intended to take big slices of cost out of GM's products. Already reeling from billions of dollars in losses, the company saw few options for cost reduction. Where would the savings come from? Competitors all showed production and material costs considerably lower than GM's, as shown by these figures published in *Business Week*:[1]

COMPARATIVE PER AUTO PRODUCTION COSTS

Toyota	$6,342
Ford	6,591
Chrysler	7,160
GM	9,068

The two major contributors to the cost of building a car are labor and materials. Labor costs include production and white-collar workers' wages; material costs include parts produced inside GM and from outside suppliers. GM's plans to close twenty-one plants would cut labor costs, but the United

Autoworkers Union, in an attempt to create job security, arranged to keep people working through the end of their expiring contract, thus preventing GM from further outsourcing.

GM procurement chose to focus cost-reduction strikes on outside suppliers, leaving the company's huge supplier network to "take the financial hit."

Lopez took several actions that puzzled suppliers. Among his first edicts was the ruling that all outstanding purchase orders over $225,000 would be "recalled" for replacement, subject to his personal Friday-afternoon review sessions. The stated reduction target was 30 to 50 percent of contracted price. Early supplier response ranged from "It won't work here" to fear that major cost reductions would happen no matter what the negative impact, to horror at the prospect of going down with the sinking giant.

Few suppliers dared speak out. One anonymous electronics supplier ("Deep Throat") commented that GM *itself* appeared to be in disarray, unsure of the new rules. Work stopped when contracts for the 1995 models were delayed; suppliers could find no one in the company willing to sign off on previous agreements. In an era in which new-product time-to-market is one of the lumbering giant's remaining competitive opportunities, suppliers no longer knew what parts, if any, they were making for GM.

"Deep Throat" continued to critique the Lopez approach, while congratulating Lopez on his tactics: "He has everybody quaking in his boots!" As to Lopez's 30 to 50 percent cost-reduction target, the supplier felt that the U.S. auto industry could not offer the same cost-cutting opportunities as Europe because "[our] margins are thinner. The European industry is run by 15 to 17 carmakers. The U.S. Big Three went through their shakeout many years ago. Most of the fat has already been trimmed."

As Ford and Chrysler tried to put a good face on their own

dealings with suppliers, giants in other industries took the opportunity to raise the hatchet with their suppliers. "Deep Throat" summarized his reaction to how the game was playing itself out: "No doubt Lopez has made an impact in a very short time. We are all reducing our prices. *The first round belongs to him.*"

FROM LEVERAGE TO PARTNERSHIP

The way GM tried to leverage its way out of operating losses generally describes the old way of working with vendors. This approach could be called "traditional purchasing practice." In this time-honored tradition, purchasing decisions are driven by leveraged negotiations. The winner uses his power—a threat of withdrawal of contracts, the promise of future business, the supplier's fear that a customer will buy from the competition, or sheer size—to get the best price, best delivery, best service, and acceptable quality from a "captive supplier."

Purchasing practice has a long history of leveraging suppliers into an agreeable position—agreeable to the purchaser. Indeed, courses on "How to Negotiate Your Best Deal" are still offered in airplane magazines and trade seminars. It's no surprise that GM and others reverted to type.

Some companies, however—like Motorola, Hewlett-Packard, and Honda of America—have matured beyond the conventional wisdom of leveraging, hammering, and negotiating their way to success on their suppliers' backs. Looking beyond short-term price objectives, they have developed procurement strategies that bring customer and supplier closer together. These companies have developed networks of strategic partnerships that will smooth the transition into the next generation of products. Drawing closer to their supplier business partners, these firms have recognized the need to depend on other companies' expertise.

Excellent companies know that a strong customer-supplier relationship generates a collective enterprise advantage. As Honda and its 256 supplier partners see it, the whole is greater than the sum of its parts. Honda's ability to assemble a high-quality competitive product from over six thousand components works because they have created a complete structure, *network manufacturing*, that integrates suppliers and the customer's assembly plants.

THE BREAKTHROUGH MATURITY PROCESS

For most companies, moving from the leveraged approach to partnering, however, is not a one-step process. A supply management organization must move along a maturity continuum that progresses from traditional purchasing practices to the advanced partnering innovation that the United States desperately needs.

From 1940 to the fat and free-wheeling sixties, U.S. manufacturers operated in multiple tiers. Big fish ate and leveraged little fish; little fish survived and prospered as best they could, fighting power tactics with appropriate price responses. During this period, the U.S. industrial landscape was neatly organized in tiers, and leverage was the commonly accepted and expected force that drove the hierarchical supply chain. Top companies squeezed their second-tier suppliers, who in turn pressured their raw material vendors.

When *volume* was king—before customers demanded quality as well as flash, before the automotive and electronics industries became commodity businesses—purchasing focused on developing a vast, captive supply network. When one vendor missed a shipment promise or raised prices, another was there to take its place. The rules were to lay out the bids, buy by price, and change suppliers when a problem appeared. Vendors knew how to play the game and protected themselves by finding creative ways to accommodate their big customers' cost drive.

A good purchasing agent "knew" his parts lists. Stuck between the guys on the floor and the occasional salesman, he was happy to

FIGURE 1.1: Supply Management Continuum

	1940–1960 TRADITIONAL PRACTICES	1970–1980	1990 PARTNERING FOR SURVIVAL, INNOVATION, AND GROWTH
Nomenclature	Purchasing	Procurement	Supply management
Organizational structure	Buyer, purchasing agent, MRP planner, vendors	Buyer/Planner	Teams: commodity, new product, project
Industry structure	Tiers ⟶		Clusters of partnering arrangements, joint ventures, customer-supplier alliances, open systems
Strategy	Cost-driven, short-term ⟶		Long-term (5 years out), total value-driven
Tactics	Leverage, multiple vendors, bid-and-quote, legal contracts, redundant inspections, limited or no information sharing, negotiations	Continuous quality improvement; supplier assessment and certification	Partnering, few suppliers, organizational boundaries blur, excellent communications, customer assessment
Reward systems	Salary, annual review based on performance to purchase-price variance		Gain sharing, team compensation plus individual compensation. Performance measured against strategic goals: timeliness, quality, service to customers.

pass the pressure on. Questionable ethical practices developed; frequently, expensive gifts sealed deals. A Long Island military aircraft purchasing manager prided himself on acquiring Cartier watches and designer luggage. A now defunct shipbuilder, careful to give the appearance of ethical buying practices, handed a supplier the keys to his trunk, stocked that morning with a case of bourbon. Purchasing managers may have argued about ethics, whether or not to let a vendor buy lunch, but the rules were different.

We have all known the pleasure at least once of being a prospective purchaser who plays car salesmen off against each other. We may even have believed they deserved it. The winner was whoever packed the most features in the lowest-cost package; that guy got the contract.

It's *almost* human nature.

A NEW GAME WITH DIFFERENT RULES—RULE 1: JIT (JUST-IN-TIME)

What would cause a customer to abandon leverage in favor of partnership and mutual continuous improvement? The three change drivers are Just-in-Time (JIT), with its heightened quality requirements; globalized competition for faster new product development; and the integration of previously separated production functions.

Purchasing can no longer stand in an isolated corner. Systems and customers demand that the supply management group participate with other business functions: engineering, customers, production, MIS (management information systems), even shipping. The only way that purchasing can meet the challenge of supplying JIT production requirements is by working with all entities in the supply chain, both suppliers and customers, to build *collective enterprise advantage.*

Collective enterprise advantage is the joining of individual company strengths into a network of partners, each contributing to the long-term growth of the enterprise. The power of the collective enterprise comes from the value of each partner's skills and resources, and the synergy that naturally happens when creative, strong contributors form an alliance. In the best alliances, partners share resources, skills, and ideas as they receive equivalent input into their own processes and products. *Breakthrough Partnering* is the process that builds collective enterprise advantage; it is a process that allows all partners to "look at both sides of the fence" and see how each partner communicates and how well each partner is internally structured to strengthen the partnership.

Collective enterprise advantage works only when each partner understands three key elements:

1. Its own goals and business interest
2. The partnering enterprise's common objectives, e.g., market share, leading-edge product development, or sheer market strength
3. Communications

As one defunct computer manufacturer discovered when he went back to a previously discarded supplier for a critically necessary plastic part, leverage and hiring and firing your vendors leave few allies for joint problem solving over the long haul.

In the 1970's, long before creating a collective enterprise advantage was even a glimmer in one executive's eye, a significant change occurred in the American industrial landscape. It was driven, as most sea changes in manufacturing are, by strong competition, this time from Japan. In the late seventies, a small green book, so badly translated from Japanese to English that it needed complete interpretation, made the rounds at Rath & Strong, a manufacturing consulting group where I worked on the design, installation, redesign, and retrofitting of MRP (Material Requirements Planning) systems. The small green book was Shigeo Shingo's book on the Toyota production system.

We were eager to read from the original, to understand the changes the Japanese had institutionalized in their car industry. In the United States, Kawasaki became the hottest example of transplanting this new technique. The idea was so new that an accurate English description of its radically different approach to manufacturing and quality and procurement was missing. It was called "JIT."

Fifteen years later, JIT is accepted practice. It has moved from the production floor to upstream and downstream operations, cutting out time and cost—waste—along the way. (Upstream functions are those located closer to the raw material source, and downstream operations are closer to final customers.) JIT forces want operations procurement to meet a far bigger challenge than that faced by production. JIT manufacturing requires procurement to arrange fast, flexible, high-quality delivery of material that supports the manufacturing drumbeat.

JIT production is one of the three drivers moving companies to Breakthrough Partnering. For many small upstream suppliers, pressure to change and improve comes from big customers like Motorola and Ford, just as those large shops have driven their *internal* suppliers to meet JIT objectives. But as the improvement focus moves farther upstream, closer and closer to the source of materials, the problems become more difficult, larger scale, and more intractable.

Why is it harder to change operations upstream than downstream? The major reason is that companies have problems tackling the "fuzzier" ways of running their business. They cannot buy a packaged system solution. Thousands of consulting dollars won't fix it, as one Midwestern pump supplier discovered after spending $6 million training an entire work force in total quality. Nor will big investments in turbo EDI, or expert systems.

The solution lies in Breakthrough Partnering. At its core, breakthrough partnering is *people*-focused, emphasizing training, developing, reorganizing, and empowering human capital to come together in teams, to partner, to build trust, to create a manufacturing network.

A division manager from one of the JIT pioneers, a Midwestern engine producer, summed up his problem this way: "It sounds so simple. Bring some people together and form teams. But it doesn't work. Can you show me how to do it?" The fact that his entire organization was structured hierarchically and that the most powerful managers with greatest longevity "didn't get it" surely explained why they had failed. Developing the people focus and the communication tools to facilitate excellent partnering is a whole new learning opportunity for many U.S. company managers.

AFTER JIT, RULE 2: PARTNERSHIPS

Breakthrough Partnering has seven drivers, all of which must be in place to support demands driven by downstream JIT production centers and to build an effective customer-supplier network.

THE SEVEN BREAKTHROUGH PARTNERING DRIVERS

1. Superior quality
2. Timeliness
3. Excellent communications
4. Flexibility
5. The attitude of continuous improvement
6. The habit of collaboration
7. Trust

The Seven Drivers are in a natural progression that companies develop as they mature in their partnering skills. The first two, superior quality and on-time delivery, are basic requirements for JIT. Drivers 3 through 6 are characteristics that excellent JIT practitioners must develop beyond JIT production. Many companies that have developed JIT have not extended it beyond the manufacturing process, but doing so is a precondition for developing the manufacturing network.

Drivers 4 through 7—flexibility, an attitude of continuous improvement, the habit of collaboration, and trust—take the organization from basic JIT competency to partnering for mutually beneficial long-term growth. Trust is the natural but difficult-to-quantify result of demonstrated proficiency in drivers one through six. In a true partnership, both partners need to be skilled in communications, flexibility, continuous improvement, and collaboration.

Advancing from basic JIT to excellent partnering is hard work. Organizations that "walk the talk" have mastered the basics and continuously practice the harder skills. Let's look at them individually.

1. Superior Quality

2. Timeliness

The first two Breakthrough Partnering drivers, superior quality and timeliness, are basic requirements for operating without waste to buffer rejected material or late shipments. Most companies have adequate systems to monitor each of these drivers. Electronics suppliers like Motorola have perfected a quality objective (fewer than 3.4 defects per million parts) they call Six Sigma that reaches all levels of their organization.

Bose Corporation is driven by its Japanese carmaker customers to deliver across one continent and the Pacific Ocean on-time, to the day. One of Bose's U.S. customers, Honda of America's

Marysville, Ohio, final assembly plant, requires hourly shipments. Although time pressures are not the same for all suppliers, Bose and others have proven that the second driver of supply excellence, timeliness, can be satisfied.

What Is Six Sigma?: Six Sigma is the name Motorola gave its quality-improvement program that seeks to keep process capabilities within a goal of 3.4 or fewer defects per million component parts. The statistical expression of this aggressive quality goal is based on a calculation of standard deviations from the average on the normal curve; six standard deviations (or sigma) representing 100 percent of the activity under the curve, means, therefore, that the process is almost 100 percent defect-free, or in perfect control.

For a purchaser, advancing beyond the first two drivers requires better-than-average performance from a supplier. Purchasing organizations can work on quality and timeliness without seriously addressing the four "fuzzier" drivers of communications, flexibility, continuous improvement, and collaboration. But for organizations to move to a fully integrated position of manufacturing and partnering excellence, they must practice and reward excellence for all seven drivers.

3. Excellent Communications

Let the data lead you.
> *Dorian Shainin, quality management pioneer and*
> *winner of the Shewhart Award*

Under the guidance of Robert Arnold, a world-class teacher, Hewlett-Packard's Andover, Massachusetts, plant has pioneered a unique approach to production meetings. Every morning production and quality personnel meet to work on current manufacturing challenges: defect issues, design questions, process points, and occasional parts shortages. The group works from a written agenda with few rules, but there is one rule that has contributed greatly to the success of these meetings: Simply, *no participant may speak without data to support his or her point.*

Motorola and HP know that without good numbers, groups work on the wrong issues. Without good data, discussions ramble off into political posturing. The old adage "Information is power" sounds better rewritten "Numbers are power." Numbers are neutral. They take the emotion out of sitting down at the table at the beginning of the partnering process.

Good communications build trust while they facilitate day-to-day activities. Immature procurement organizations operating under traditional practices do not deliberately share or systematically measure and report their requirements or activities. But a data-driven approach to communications makes companies like Motorola and Hewlett-Packard good partners.

Unfortunately, even leaders in excellence must struggle with the technical aspects of communications. EDI, paperless transfer of data, bulletin boards, measurement and rating systems—all are simply communications vehicles, devices to help potential partners sit down at the table. The technology that enables partners to build a complete electronic open system network is here; pioneering applications will be available by 1995. Although the transfer of ordinary data like forecasts may be awkward, and in fact requires much human intervention, most companies can track the few basic numbers that will enable their enterprise partners to speak with confidence about costs, quality, and delivery requirements.

Good communications also extend beyond the factory walls to customers. John Gilbertson, president of AVX, a Myrtle Beach components supplier, followed the kickoff of his internal Quality Vision 2000 program with a customer survey. Sent to more than three thousand customers, the questionnaire sought to determine how customers viewed various service features such as on-time delivery, service, technical literature, and communications.

Why would a supplier seek feedback from a customer like Motorola? Fifteen years ago, when Gilbertson started in the business, he faced thirty-three competitors. That lineup has been cut down to fewer than twelve viable contenders, half of which are overseas. Customers like IBM and others carry less inventory and introduce more new products faster; they need heightened flexibility and product variety. Further, their supply base has been radically reduced by the disappearance of less "fit" companies.

In this competitive climate, U.S. manufacturing has moved through a series of "umbrella solutions," from operations research to MRP and MRP II. The current "one-size-fits-all" solution, Total Quality, has expanded far beyond the original scope proposed by quality leaders Dorian Shainin, Deming, and Juran. Big systems and Total Quality drives do not form the basis for better partnerships. At their heart, *partnerships are made by people* working to create an entirely new level of enterprise advantage.

Over the last several years, the landscape of manufacturing has been redrawn as clusters of customer-supplier groups replace the rusted-out giants. Tentative connections, finely penciled lines linking supplier and user are forming a pattern of strategic linkages. As each new line is drawn, another partnership develops. Let's look at how these new collaborations are taking down the walls separating potential partners.

Customers sometimes inadvertently set up barriers for suppliers, for example, when they encounter inconsistency in a customer's procurement practices from one department to another. Good partners, whether their business is purchasing, finance, or engineering, are consistent in the way they treat their suppliers. Dave Nelson of Honda calls this philosophy "same face," an image drawn from a Japanese spaghetti-like candy called Kintori Amay, or Kinton, after an ancient Samurai warrior named Kintori. No matter where you cut a cross-section, you see the same outline of a human face!

The way customers and suppliers communicate beyond their initial collaboration agreement determines how strong and effective the partnership becomes. In these partnerships, numbers force the players to turn subjective comments, reactions, and feelings into actionable goals. Williams Technologies, a South Carolina remanufacturer of automotive transmissions partnering with GM Powertrain, developed a simple rating system in response to GM's supplier assessment. Although Williams's system is less detailed than GM's document, it presents a simple five-step system for rating Williams' performance.

4. Flexibility

Flexibility in excellent partnerships is epitomized by the Boeing-United agreement that solved several 777 Aircraft design and development challenges.

As a supplier, Boeing is concerned with on-time deliveries, manufacturing cost, and many design issues that previously would not have been exposed to partners. Boeing customers, whose profitability hinges on rapid and clean turnaround service times, complained that the electronics bay hatch-cover design could cause accidents. The partnership solution was to relocate the access door, thereby eliminating accident potential, without adding manufacturing cost or aerodynamic drag. Each partner to the compromise agreement demonstrated a willingness to be flexible. Both companies responded to the challenge by dedicating high-level engineers from both sides of the table to joint design teams.

On the other hand, partnering can be a difficult challenge for rule-bound organizations that prefer to operate by the rules for "the sake of the rules."

5. An Attitude of Continuous Improvement

> Our customers make us get better.
> *Lance Dixon, director of purchasing and logistics, Bose Corporation*

Small companies like Bose, a manufacturer of high-end speaker systems, often partner with large, mature organizations like Honda and Nissan. Such partnerships enable smaller companies to make quantum leaps in meeting their customers' aggressive quality and delivery standards. Where hi-fi supplier Bose might have satisfied the market with cosmetically and technically superior equipment, it has been forced to innovate in logistics as well, to meet tougher partnership demands.

Honda of America (HAM) is another very demanding Bose customer. Located in Marysville, Ohio, Honda requires daily just-in-time deliveries of stereo systems. If Bose misses a scheduled shipment to Honda by more than one-half a shift, the problem is noted on the supplier's report card that Honda keeps and is sent directly to Sherwin Greenblatt, Bose's president.

At its very best, the habit of continuous improvement is contagious as smaller companies model themselves after their customers. Simpson Industries, a North Carolina machining supplier to Consolidated Diesel, mirrors the latter's style in uniforms, measurement systems, and shop housekeeping, down to stripes painted on the floor, in a concrete demonstration of their shared interest in mutual improvement.

6. The Habit of Collaboration

It is easier to approach future partners for teaming if your company has first practiced joint work efforts inside the company. Mature organizations that develop strong collaboration skills internally with project teams, quality improvement drives, and other group efforts have a natural inclination toward collaboration with outsiders. Good collaborations get recognition; team members are rewarded for working with other functions, for learning new languages and cultures, and for crossing or removing boundaries. Management encourages team members to move to the next team effort by rewarding their efforts, and sets an example itself through partnering with other companies and professional associations.

How far does this habit of collaboration go? In one East Coast temperature controls manufacturer, every employee has been involved in at least six improvement or problem-solving teams per year, some with outside partners. At Motorola/Codex of Mansfield, Massachusetts, there are currently fifty-four self-directed work teams, representing 40 percent of the three thousand–person workforce. These initiatives are critically important to creating an internal climate where outside collaboration will flourish.

7. Trust

The "fuzziest" term of the Seven Breakthrough Partnering Drivers is *trust*. Although it is easy to identify actions that destroy trust, companies need to understand specific actions that build it. Some companies mature technically by building solid quality systems, by integrating various planning and control systems, but when it comes to trust, they fail by cautiously approaching the goal of deliberately developing trust. Managers hesitate, phrasing their doubts in a series of questions about how to build trust in partnerships: What should we do? How far should we go? How much of this "trust business" depends on legal protection, or contractual agreements?

Start with day-to-day operating issues at the "basic JIT" end of the maturity index. When companies perfect JIT scheduling and reduce inventory levels, they must trust suppliers to keep their operations running. GM manages many of its facilities on a JIT delivery schedule. But the company learned during the recent Lordstown strike that *trust is not a line item in the contract*. When a parts plant struck and shut down several final-assembly vehicle lines, it demonstrated the risk of operating a system as demanding as JIT in an adversarial labor-management environment.

Companies such as Honda and Motorola that excel in partnering work hard to build trust around specific issues. When they succeed, they are credited with "walking the talk." When they fail, they work on the root causes of the failure. Supplier councils, resource grants to small suppliers to help with difficult issues like environmental regulations, supplier awards, and benchmarking projects tell Honda's suppliers that, although Honda demands a great deal, "Honda wants them to do well because when they do well, we do well," according to Dave Nelson, Honda of America's vice president of purchasing.

Any operation serious about extending its power beyond the factory walls can learn to partner, and trust lies at the heart of all partnering activities. Team-based cultures like those at Honda and Hewlett-Packard adopt the new rules quickly, but it's not difficult to understand why some groups skilled at business "football" would find it hard to throw out the rulebook and win track relays. By perfecting the Seven Breakthrough Partnering Drivers, any company, regardless of size, can learn to partner.

From the beginning, companies must let go of old practices. Leveraging and other win-lose tactics won't draw on the best skills of both partners. If it's your intent to build a network of strategically linked partners, you should avoid adversarial activities like purchase-price variance awards and bid-and-quote selection.

Motorola and Molex, Honda and LTV Steel, Xerox and Seitz corporations, Apple and Solectron, EMC Corporation and Seagate, Nypro and Johnson & Johnson Vistakon have developed partnerships that go beyond the consumption of a supplier's material. These customer partners draw on their suppliers' expertise and critical skills to improve their own products. Who, for example, would know more about quality or cosmetic performance of plastic speaker cabinets than the plastics supplier? Who is better able to design an aircraft that facilitates fast turnarounds and smooth servicing than the customers who actually perform the maintenance? Boeing and its customer partners, ANA (All Nippon Airways) and United Airlines, work hard to incorporate service and cosmetic improvements, as well as to meet technical and cost objectives.

Partnering for mutual advantage is a significant challenge, for it requires all Seven Breakthrough Partnering Drivers. To genuinely partner, key suppliers and customers' organizations must excel at all of the seven vital practices, not just one or a few. GM may excel at quality, and certainly within GM there are unsung heros who risk retribution by trying to maintain good partnering practices. But without the habit of collaboration, and communications to support that habit, GM is doomed to performing the old way.

Big old organizations like GM often use all the right words— *partnership, sharing, trust, Total Value*—but fall back on leverage to force concessions from unwilling supplier "partners." GM further complicates suppliers' lives with a flurry of certification and recertification audits, each one different, requiring resources that small businesses cannot afford to waste. No wonder small businesses seek out new customers!

The American industrial landscape, which once appeared as a system of neat, clear hierarchies, looks very different as various partnerships form and grow. Bill Hanson, former vice president of manufacturing at Digital Equipment Corporation, described the new view as looking through a microscope at a drop of pond water. Dubbed "pond scum," his vision of this living universe showed many new working arrangements bubbling up, some of which develop into robust partnerships while others dissolve in the heat of day. Some partners come together to collaborate on new product development. Others become an information-sharing forum.

Companies like Baldrige Award winner Motorola admit that

they cannot achieve excellence all by themselves. As a result, they changed the rules. Realizing that the new partnerships are not based on leverage or bribery, or winners and losers, they redrew their vision to be organic, much like former Digital VP Bill Hanson's "pond scum," dotted with strategic linkages. Not only does the landscape look different, but the new breakthrough partners work differently from their predecessors.

BUILDING THE PARTNERSHIP BRIDGE

Excellent partners communicate effectively and frequently inside their own organizations as well as with their partners. To build a bridge linking customers with suppliers, spanning all the possible contingencies that arise in competitive markets, breakthrough partners must build a strong support structure. All of the Seven Drivers supporting the partnership bridge must be in place.

Changing an immature organization driven by leverage and negotiation with suppliers, a win-lose approach, may be too frightening for many companies. And some people who have mastered traditional purchasing skills simply choose not to change.

Establishing new linkages based on the concept of equal partners certainly requires patience. There are few "quick hits" and even fewer "surgical strikes." Being honest about product and process requirements and capabilities takes practice, but the proven benefits will take strong partners into the next century, which promises bloody competition between clusters of networked manufacturers.

BREAKTHROUGH PARTNERING BENEFITS

The six benefits of Breakthrough Partnering are clear to partners like Honda, Motorola, Solectron, Nypro, and EMC:

Figure 1.2: The Customer-Supplier Partnership Bridge

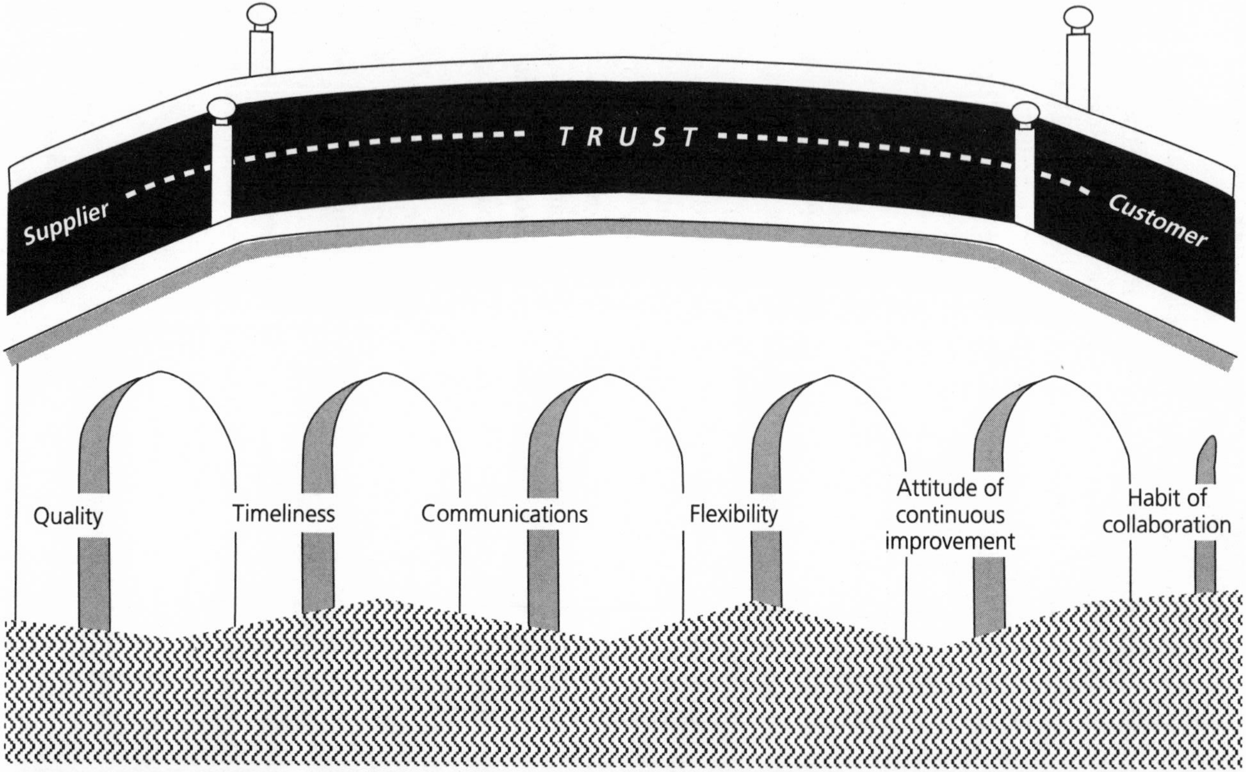

1. Faster time-to-market
2. Improved design
3. Improved quality
4. Greater responsiveness
5. Flexibility
6. Lower costs

The partnership that Solectron and PictureTel, a Massachusetts teleconferencing systems producer, have developed has enabled PictureTel to fund its "market window." Suppliers' expertise has led to a stronger PictureTel product. Partnering with PictureTel has given Solectron another opportunity to establish a beachhead on the East Coast. Other benefits of strategic partnering abound. Many small GM suppliers are scrambling to hire new customers who will supplement their resources with leading-edge technology, and offer training and development, as does Honda's BP (Best Partner Supplier Development) program.

GM has learned the hard way the lesson that *JIT doesn't work with half a team*. Without its network of parts suppliers making synchronous deliveries of components like seats and radios, Honda's Marysville Accord assembly plant would shut down.

THE IMPORTANCE OF REMOVING BARRIERS

At a 1992 meeting of the Association for Manufacturing Excellence's Customer Supplier Partnership Team (CUSSUPS), two breakout groups worked for an afternoon listing the barriers blocking customer-supplier linkages. Of the hundreds of barriers identified—lack of management support, scheduling problems, emphasis on cost and not value—the majority related to communications and trust. (Specific cases will be discussed in later chapters.)

Many barriers to communications have begun to crumble, and communications will continue to improve as more companies adopt simple communications tools and as open systems become a reality. It is important to remember that numbers are an aspect of every partnership transaction. Improved communications and better data will result from partnerships where team participants include other functional representatives: finance, accounting, manufacturing, and human resources. They are the source of vital numbers without which the partnership founders.

Taking down the walls is the first step to good partnering, but it is not enough. To be a true partner, companies must be as good as they expect their suppliers to be. (Baldrige winner Motorola asks all its suppliers to apply for the award.) Good partners help their teammates by removing barriers, building bridge supports, and developing *touchpoints*—strategic contact points into which a potential partner can connect. The touchpoints may be people in your company designated as key communicators, or problem solvers for customers, or they may be conduits to quality communications. Such people can solve a problem frequently cited by suppliers and customers alike without being handed off from one functional silo to another.

For example, partnerships can also founder on complex, multi-layered supply chains, and so before building bridges good partners first simplify their supply chain, concentrating their growth efforts on a few suppliers, a few key partnership projects. The supply chain for a typical high-tech start up assembling mass storage devices illustrates this principle.

In Figure 1.3a the product first comes together through a number of steps that add cost, time, and confusion to the cycle. Figure 1.3b, a simplified supply chain, shows product assembled at the end of a clear supply line, having moved down a shorter supply chain. In Figure 1.3b, the final producer has abandoned most vertical integration and moved closer upstream to the expert producers: the board houses and memory experts.

The restructured computer industry proves how end customers

FIGURE 1.3: Supply Chain Simplification

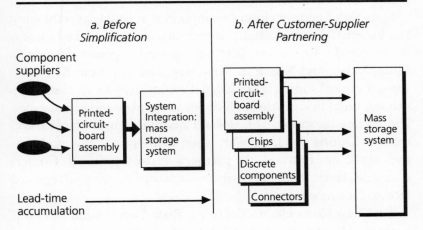

drive assemblers to work faster and leaner, forcing big final assembly houses like Digital Equipment Company, IBM, and even Sun Microsystems to get closer to their suppliers.

New partnering arrangements are born daily as the pressure to partner for enterprise advantage comes from all sides. *L.A. Times* industry analyst Michael Shrage argues that many of the reasons behind partnering in high tech derive from individual developers' limited access to massive funding for capital investment, research, and new product development; survivors have no choice but to pool resources.

Bridges to Suppliers

The first step in removing barriers is perfecting quality and other "technical" product or process performance. Most customers start with vendor certification and reduction of the supply base to select manufacturing network partners. In the network environment, however, partners initially focus on qualification, selection, and feedback systems. But world-class supply management, looking at both sides of the fence, takes partnership beyond the technical issues.

Sometimes getting closer to suppliers is as simple as rethinking the logistics. Plant location, or network design, is a key success factor for the new green-field auto assembly plants: Honda in Ohio, Saturn and Nissan in Tennessee, and Toyota in Kentucky. Even if critical suppliers are located a continent away, customers can still build bridges through co-location, plant visits, and excellent communications. This doesn't necessarily mean large travel outlays: During the Gulf War, when many procurement executives chose not to travel, the partnership still continued. Conference calls, faxes, bulletin boards, and teleconferencing all replaced face-to-face meetings.

Two East Coast electronics firms, Bose Corporation of Framingham, Massachusetts, and EMC of nearby Hopkinton, have designed innovative bridges to their critical suppliers. Both invite suppliers to work in-house with purchasing and handle day-to-day operations issues. Bose's in-plant reps replace the salesperson and the buyers for nine commodity areas, ranging from printing, plastics, and metal stampings to transportation. The goal is to shrink the supply cycle and build closer relationships and trust between customer and supplier experts. EMC's "in-plants" accomplish the same goals: to improve communications and trust and to draw on specific expertise that typically resides with suppliers.

The vision of strong partners meeting to collaborate requires each partner to put aside much of what has previously been accepted as standard business practice.

A survey conducted in 1992 by the Association for Manufacturing Excellence (AME) asked suppliers to identify the characteristics that define a good customer and those that destroy a developing relationship. These are the skills that suppliers cited on their "customer wish list":

- Early supplier involvement
- Mutual trust
- Involvement in product design
- Quality initiatives
- Profitability
- Schedule sharing
- Responsiveness to cost reduction ideas
- Communications and feedback
- Crisis management response
- Commitment to partnership

Respondents summarized the actions that derailed partnerships. A steel marketing executive talked about "the customer who talks quality and service, and then buys on price alone." A sales manager in fasteners describes a poor partner as one who "uses all the buzzwords in the industry, expects a formal presentation to meet his needs, then makes a final decision by price alone and ignores previous statements." Another describes a bad customer as one that relies on "sealed bid quotes, has a price-only mentality, leverages one supplier against another, and shows a lack of creativity and foresight in determining mutual direction!"

World-Class Customers Need World-Class Suppliers

Customers and suppliers who want to become strong partners need to develop the critical skills that support the Seven Partnership Drivers. These companies develop systems that support partnering activities—from people-oriented systems to management structures that make partnering easier to technical systems that cut through detail to quality systems that build better products.

Excellent partnering benefits both parties. Motorola has recognized that to continue its Six Sigma objectives it must be an excellent customer. Its partner suppliers must also commit themselves to aggressive quality-improvement targets, if not Six Sigma, then certainly exponential improvements, as in the case of connector manufacturer Molex.

Good customers collaborate for specific projects only, while world-class customers have adopted the habit of collaboration in all spheres. What distinguishes the best customers from the average? Ford Motor Company was named as one of the former because "they know their needs and choose partners after careful analysis."

ALMOST PARTNERS

Reflect on the story of an East Coast controls producer, Controls, Inc. The product is an electronic assembly housed in a metal frame cast by a Midwest manufacturer, Midwest Casting. All deliveries had been flowing on schedule and at acceptable quality levels until the casting house made some organizational changes and moved to a new building. Although it taxed the company's patience, the customer stayed with his supplier, and within six months deliveries were back on track.

Recently, however, quality problems have alarmed Controls, Inc. Rather than drop Midwest Casting and build a relationship with a new supplier, Controls, Inc.'s purchasing manager pulled together a team for an on-site visit at Midwest Casting.

For two days the Controls, Inc. team visited, talked, and walked through Midwest Casting's plant. Having already adopted internal team improvement procedures such as CEDAC (cause-and-effect diagram with the addition of cards) and group problem solving, they felt empowered to assist at Midwest Casting. The team's visit resulted in a six-page trip report, which amounted to free management consulting.

A letter from Dave, Control, Inc.'s purchasing manager and team scribe, included general observations that took the company's pulse: "Midwest Casting, Inc., appeared to be more organized than . . . on the previous visit. Aisles were clear . . . work appeared to move from one work station to the next in a structured fashion."

Management practices were scrutinized: "Management appeared to have a fairly close relationship with the work force. The people seemed at ease around their supervisors (and guests) and readily answered any questions."

"The attitude at Midwest Casting, Inc., was very positive. People seemed to want to get better and there was evidence of different things being tried to achieve that goal."

Specific issues with finance, shipment-tracking problems, and an awkward mix of manual and computerized operations in the shipping/invoicing system were reviewed. The team even offered to lend its supplier some computer talent.

So far so good. The recommendations continue through each critical production area, and the list of constructive criticisms builds:

- Die casting done on the first floor, materials move to the second floor for machining.
- Freight elevators break down.
- Castings wait too long to cool; would quench tanks between operations improve throughput?
- Would a U-cell layout cut transport time and tie separate machine operators closer to each other?
- Are operators trained to control gauging?
- We love your attention to quality, but would it make more sense to train operators in quality, rather than adding inspectors???

How did Midwest Casting take it? There is nothing harder to receive than the gift of free advice. Charlie, the president, agreed with some of the recommendations. He replied that he was "doing my best to be humble, with a master's degree in industrial engineering, and having taught at the university level, before becoming a management consultant for 15 years before 'going straight.' " Yet Dave sensed a shift from listening to resisting improvement suggestions. Charlie recounted that each specific recommendation was now in the hands of a production manager. Indeed, he said, many of the solutions were already in place! As to improving quality by training operators, he insisted that "this is too extensive a subject to be dealt with superficially. . . . we have undertaken an extensive analysis of our entire program."

Sadly, Dave and Charlie ended up *almost partners*. Each needed the other's help; both ended up with less than they wanted. Could the story have had a different ending? Other potential partners might have initiated the partnership at their own level, rather than being drawn into it by a group of well-meaning practitioners. The communications might have been handled differently, namely, on a day-to-day operating basis, instead of via a sweeping, all-encompassing document. In this way, communications and trust would have been developed slowly throughout their organizations, or at least at the critical contact points.

The recurrent and crucial questions are: How can one communicate effectively? What kinds of questions and recommendations are most likely to improve old practices? Will suppliers listen to big customers? Sure—but will they change?

TRUE PARTNERS

Everybody wants to "do teams." Everyone wants an in-house design team, or a cross-functional design team, or a self-directed work team, or a continuous improvement team, or a strategic customer-supplier team, Donna Neusch, coauthor of *The High Performance Enterprise*, says that two-thirds of all teams fail. We need models for the very special integration of customers and suppliers. Breakthrough Partnering offers potential partners new, simple communications tools to bring companies together and build trust, and new assessment and evaluation instruments to build strong linkages.

In the partnering examples that follow—Boeing, United, and ANA; Solectron and PictureTel; Motorola and Molex; EMC and Seagate—the partnering process takes time and cost out of operations and increases flexibility while creating more robust product designs. The exercise of sitting down and setting mutually advantageous goals may be unsettling, but the process of reaching agreement teaches both parties much about themselves.

Trust and good communications, powerful but "soft" descriptions of the foundation for strong partnerships, have not been easy for most supply managers to develop. But companies that recognize the necessity of strong partners for the long haul can develop powerful partnering skills. As companies move ahead and develop new practices, they will become more flexible and capable of drawing on the strengths of their partners.

Partners must be as excellent as they expect their team members to be, with the requisite internal strengths: strategic vision, management support, excellent communications, organization structure, people systems, a world-class procurement organization, and partnering strengths to move across the bridge from adversarial relationships to world-class partnerships.

NOTES

1. Clyde V. Prestowitz, Jr., quoted in "Detroit's Big Chance," *Business Week*, June 29, 1992, p. 84.

CHAPTER **2**

Beyond Continuous Improvement and Total Quality

*T*he first time I saw Bill Mackenzie he was hammering the new roof on a center-entrance Colonial that three weeks earlier had been a quaint white Cape Cod cottage. It was February, and the thermometer had been stuck at 30° below for five days. Bill wore a hooded sweatshirt with the drawstring pulled tight around his face, and no gloves. They would interfere with The Work. The pockets of his down parka were filled with tools.

My spouse and I had been talking with contractors, exploring how to get one step closer to our dream house. The first contractor pointed to my lovely Mont Morency cherry tree out back and explained that it would have to go to make room for the extension; he advised against going up. The second, a local boy, recommended six months' work, starting with gutting the current residence.

It seemed to me that this kind of potentially catastrophic project required a special kind of builder, a workaholic with whom we could share bathroom and kitchen privileges. Someone who would finish the job quickly with a crew who could be trusted to feed the cat and lock the door.

We invited Bill, who later acquired the nickname "Wild Bill, the JIT contractor," to visit and scope out the project. We sat at the kitchen table. It was simple. We talked; he sketched. He explained the conditions of our partnership. We would go for the vanilla Yankee approach, eschewing fancy moldings, Jacuzzis, and cathedral ceilings; he would promise to be done and out in six weeks, in time for our anniversary open house. We could if necessary draw up a legal contract and take it to our attorney. He supplied a list of references, other householders who had experienced The Work. He scratched an estimate on the back of a business card and slipped it into his wallet (his thick backlog file). He was booked eight months out, but if we were willing to wait and to keep the architects out of it, we could get our dream house for 60 percent of the other low bid.

We decided to wait. Time passed; our impatience built daily. The zoning variance came through with no hitches and we had time to get our finances ready for the big hit.

Bill's plan for the project required a three-day window with no rain. During those three days he would simultaneously rip off the old roof and build the framework for the new one. Advance planning was terribly important. There would be a twenty-four-to-forty-eight-hour period when the house would resemble a box with a tarp cover. Bill preferred the winter months for The Work—light snow was better than spring rains and October hurricanes.

All materials were scheduled to arrive one day before the start. A full crew of five, each dedicated to one section of the house, would work twelve-to-fourteen-hour days for the first week. After the new roof frame was up and covered with plywood, Bill and his crew would cut back to eight-plus hours a day.

We knew the time had come on a Sunday in February when we noticed Bill driving back and forth in front of our little house in his restored Model A truck, slowing as he leaned out to better view his next victim. Clearly, this was a man with a mission. When we heard the *ar-r-ruga* horn, we knew there was no turning back.

Here's where the real heart of our partnership—trust and confidence in Bill's abilities—takes hold. Living in a house with plaster ceilings as the only barrier between you and a New England winter sky is a "unique" experience. Some folks take off for Disney World and come back to the finished product. But we trusted Bill. For us, legal contracts, late penalties, and completion bonds were meaningless. They could never really compensate for poor planning.

Bill had it all in his head, from where to cut the hole to push fiberglas tub units through the second-floor walls to when to bring in the heating, plumbing, electrical, and masonry subcontractors. It was a wonderful experience—I would do it again without hesitation, but only with Wild Bill, the JIT Contractor. It was interesting watching the crew hammer away. As long as we stayed out of their way, things moved quickly. Within a week we had a new roof, and in three more weeks the walls were in place. All decisions, down to the color of the fixtures, were made in advance. Only little decisions that would not delay The Work were presented to us as each new step in the operation appeared.

JIT manufacturing doesn't tolerate waste; Bill lived by the same principle. Any lumber that he could recycle from the old frame was used on the new one. It saved trucking perfectly good materials to the dump, where we would be charged a dump fee. Although the design was simple, it was adequate for our needs.

We mounted in a frame the ultimate sign of trust: the $1' \times 2'$ wallboard scrap outlining the total costs and basics on which we sealed the deal. There was no other legal agreement.

Bill's approach to The Work can be summarized as follows:

1. The way to make money is to plan it, do it, finish it, and go on to the next project. *Planning is 80 percent of The Work.*

2. Train the crew.
3. Recycle where you can.
4. Don't work with people you can't work with. Make customers for life, your next good reference. *Pick your customers carefully.*
5. Avoid the waste inherent in indebtedness and excess inventory or people. Frugal Yankee Bill built the business not on leverage, but on the one-inch stack of estimates scribbled on business cards—his backlog file that tells him how well he's doing.

JIT AND BEYOND

> We're out of the woods. The scope of this next phase of manufacturing is what makes it hard.
> *Robert W. Hall, 1993*

Supply chain partners, whether they are internal or external customers and suppliers, are affected by downstream production methods, no matter what techniques and philosophies—JIT, Total Quality Management (TQM), lean manufacturing, or MRP II (second-generation MRP)—drive them. Every downstream effort to cut waste and improve quality will benefit from the support of like-minded upstream supply management approaches. When supply management professionals understand the evolution of manufacturing management techniques, they will be better equipped to work with their downstream customers and with their upstream suppliers on critical control issues such as inventory management, scheduling, quality, and flexibility.

In the fifteen or so years that U.S. companies have been consciously working on developing new manufacturing approaches, they have moved at very different tempos, just as one would expect. Some companies have been anxious to discard all signs of the old manufacturing techniques such as big inventories, expediting, and manual control systems. They have ripped out the big MRP systems, shut down automated warehouses, and moved machinery around to simpler, cleaner flows. Others have taken a more conservative approach, trying to layer new approaches on older ones. Few have had the advantage of starting up fresh on a green field site, with compensation systems and MIS systems, manufacturing processes, and layouts all developed to work perfectly together.

Let's look at the recent evolution of manufacturing planning and control systems. We'll call the current picture of industry "post-JIT, post-TQM," because both philosophies have been around long enough to have affected every aspect of manufacturing, but not long enough to thoroughly influence areas outside production.

Our current blend of manufacturing techniques—post-JIT, post-TQM enterprise integration—first of all assumes that quality levels are high. Superior quality, like Motorola's Six Sigma quality program, is the base requirement for being in the game, the entrance fee. And JIT's dedication to manufacturing guru Richard Schonberger's "attitude of continuous improvement" has taken hold: Everyone is *thinking* of "getting better"; inventory and other waste is bad; people, our real assets, need opportunities to grow. Organizations have become flatter and more flexible.

Compensation systems are still a puzzle. We have a range of individual compensation schemes, and team compensation is being done in dozens of ways. Outsourcing and subcontracting will only grow in importance as companies like IBM "destructure," and vertical integration is replaced with linkages of customers and suppliers.

The status and practice of partnering is clearly uneven in American industry. Various aspects of partnering are being tried in some industries, but a few very visible models involve applying leverage and clout to "partners," resulting in networks of forced marriages, not true partnerships.

Let's take a look back to the developments and ideas that have laid the groundwork for today's partnering opportunities.

FIGURE 2.1: The Evolution of Manufacturing Control Systems

PRODUCTION PLANNING AND CONTROL				ENTERPRISE INTEGRATION
1950s	1960s	1970s	1980s	1990s
Reorder point planning; Min/Max Time-phased reorder point planning Lot sizes, algorithm	Mainframe computers with punch card, Limited MRP	Full MRP, Shop floor control, Computer-generated purchase orders	Manufacturing excellence: TQM, JIT, Networked computer systems	Customer-supplier teams linked by open networked systems

THE 1960s: THE ERA OF THE MAINFRAME

With the creation of its bill of materials (BOM) processor, IBM ushered in the age of production applications of computers, the operations research approach to scheduling. Companies used their mainframes for specific planning jobs: MRP, BOM, order scheduling, purchasing paperwork control systems. Systems that handled payroll would be diverted to other number-crunching applications. Planning was in the hands of a few production managers supported by number crunchers and expediters. The power and fascination of the computer, however, was taking hold: "Any problem can be calculated out."

The distance between the shop floor and office/white-collar managers grew with the consolidation and growth of the white-collar bureaucracy: the men with the corner window offices, the office girls, all working for the promise of reserved parking and the penthouse. Management divvied up the spoils, the most profitable chunks of the business, and each middle manager got an office, a secretary, a chair with arms. Shop people stayed on the floor and office people stayed at their desks.

THE 1970s: MRP CRUSADES AND THE JIT REVOLUTION

Full-blown MRP II systems covered the entire production function. These systems were viewed by most companies as a scheduling tool. MRP II integrated capacity planning and some "what-if" capabilities, promising to tie all customer order, finished goods, and component scheduling and forecasting questions into one big system.

In 1978 an APICS (American Production and Inventory Control Society) special interest group, the Repetitive Manufacturing Group, ran a $50-a-head workshop on JIT at the Kawasaki plant in Nebraska. Attendees were energized and became the "happy band of missionaries" who popularized JIT in the United States: Robert W. "Doc" Hall, author of *Zero Inventories* (originally titled *Stockless Production*); Ed Hay, then of Fram, who visited Japan and described their radical reduction of setup times; Richard Schonberger, then at the University of Nebraska; Nick Edwards and Bill Wheeler from Rath & Strong; and others.

A few companies took up the challenge to reduce inventories and rearrange production lines, as well as demand higher-quality, right-the-first-time work. Hewlett-Packard in Colorado, Harley-Davidson, Briggs & Stratton, and a handful of others Americanized the ideas they had gleaned from the Kawasaki workshop, the little green Shingo book, and well-publicized trips to Japan. The battle was on!

THE 1980s: MANUFACTURING EXCELLENCE

> Turn up your hearing aid—it ain't "On Golden Pond"!
> *Remark made by wife of factory owner, both attending one of the 135 JIT presentations "Doc" Hall made in 1984, at the Arizona Biltmore*

In 1985 APIC's Repetitive Manufacturing Group became the Association for Manufacturing Excellence (AME). "JIT," originally a part of AME's new name, was later dropped. AME shifted the focus from inventory reduction, a misreading of JIT principles, to total enterprise improvement and world-class quality.

Work-force development, cross-functional training, and cross-functional teams began to dissolve the "functional silos." Companies rediscovered the customer.

Procurement pioneers formed commodity teams and widened skills sets in organizations that had to supply the downstream JIT customer. Xerox, under tremendous competitive pressures, pioneered supply base management.

THE 1990s: THE INTEGRATED ENTERPRISE

The early JIT crusades were a threat to traditional thinking, because as JIT crusaders urged reduced inventories, they laid bare layers of paperwork, people, and inventory that covered mistakes. Likewise, the idea of partnering with suppliers represented a threat to many purchasing professionals, even though partnering is essential to draw on the best resources of suppliers and customers. The integrated enterprise is characterized by open systems with "plug and play" characteristics, and fewer but better-trained and more flexible employees than the contrasting white-collar and blue-collar professionals of the sixties.

Most organizations have integrated some aspects of Just-in-Time philosophy into their production operations, although they may not have moved beyond the factory floor. In fact, purchasing typically is the last function to be integrated into a JIT manufacturing system, after production and quality functions have been upgraded. This is a curious approach to improving production operations, considering the impact the front end, procurement, has on all downstream scheduling.

The objectives of excellent JIT manufacturing are as follows:

- The elimination of waste throughout the organization
- Superior quality
- Low costs
- Short lead times
- An attitude of continuous improvement
- Excellent customer service

Each of these objectives has supporting methodologies. The methods for achieving superior quality, for example, include Design of Experiments, Statistical Process Control, Taguchi methods, and supplier certification. But unlike other manufacturing management planning and control techniques that have appeared since the first applications of scientific management to production, JIT is not another *technique*. It is a *philosophy* based on improvement of various enterprise functions.

JIT is *not*

- An inventory control program, although it does foster reduction of lot sizes, removal of safety stocks, and elimination of queues
- An attempt to force suppliers to carry buffer inventory that is removed from the consuming production facility
- A purely cultural change process, although JIT does indeed emphasize team-based improvement efforts
- A replacement for MRP

Reduction of design and production defects allows JIT practitioners to remove buffer inventories wherever they appear in the process. JIT simplifies quality assurance methods and places them in the hands of production associates.

By concentrating on smooth, uninterrupted material flows or linearity, JIT allows producers to optimize production processes. Benefits include reduced overtime, expediting, and premium freight charges. JIT production managers want to focus only on flexibility requirements.

Supply management can, by establishing strong supplier networks, stop, adjust, and improve the supply chain. Working with production facilities outside the factory walls then becomes standard practice. A key measure of success is the extent to which product moves in a smooth flow, from the beginning of the process through to shipping. Linearity, or uniform plant flow, requires material to be delivered in predictable, regular patterns ("the drumbeat"), as near perfectly synchronized with consuming plants as possible. Even as production switches over to new products, the factory seeks to maintain linearity and to eliminate disruptions that might lead to the accumulation of inventory or other waste.

Partnered customers and suppliers contribute to linearity by managing supplier agreements and transport schedules that accommodate, wherever possible, the uninterrupted inflow of materials. If the assembly plant consumes at 45 rpm, the suppliers must also run at 45 rpm, not 78 rpm. If the supplier runs at 33⅓ rpm, there will be shortages.

The JIT crusade and the quality crusade that followed gave us a new production vocabulary, including:

kanban
backflushing
visual management
Hoshin Kanri planning
QFD (Quality Function Deployment)
CEDAC
Taguchi
empowerment
cross-functional
Design of Experiments
commodity team
lot sizes of one

The beginning of the nineties saw terms like "agile manufacturing" and "lean production" take hold. These visions have been difficult to describe because they are still only visions. There are few models of complete, integrated enterprises to examine. Although in retrospect it is easy to see how production methods changed and to understand the contributions of various innovators at each stage, seeing into the future is a challenge. The auto industry illustrates movement from a machine shop in a garage out back, to Henry Ford's consolidation of the industry in his high-volume, low-variety production concept, to Toyota's Three-Day Car concept. The implications for supply management throughout these changes are enormous.

In *The Reckoning* David Halberstam predicted overcapacity of vehicle supply by the year 1990, a buyer's market. The response of auto competitors resembles the old game of chicken. Each competitor recognized the abundance of supply, but refused to back out of the game and held on to excess factories well beyond the point of creating a profitability dilemma. The attitude seemed to be that to "pull out," guaranteed a loss of market share. When you lose your seat in musical chairs, you are out of the game forever. Even the winners, those who grab a seat when the music stops, find staying in the game a continuous challenge.

PEERING INTO THE FUTURE

It's probable that the auto industry as we know it will no longer exist in a few years. Ford's assembly-line approach to high-volume auto manufacturing took out the custom low-volume shops and set the standard for good production techniques for decades. The "new Henry Ford" has not made an appearance yet, but we can be assured that his or her factory won't look like anything we have seen so far. The new auto assembly plant might consist of three smaller factories: (1) a customer design room with a CAD/CAM workstation linked to (2) a staging area where new body panels, seats, and other components arrive from suppliers, and (3) immediately next to staging, the final assembly area from which the customer drives away, a few days after her appointment with the sales/design associate.

Think about what it takes to supply this new manufacturing

enterprise, which we will call Global People Movers, Inc. (GPM). Because GPM offers customers the opportunity to design their own model on a standard frame a commonly well-managed production sequencing problem will be instantaneously communicated to suppliers. Other components, also customized by the buyer, will have "plug and play" characteristics typically seen in the computer industry. All material suppliers will have been certified for direct delivery to the staging or final assembly area. It also means that certified, valued partners will design a large portion of the finished car; concept paperwork goes to the sole winners of the design (formerly bid) competition.

Total cost to produce the vehicle will have dropped, as will the portion representing labor costs. Reduced labor costs will still include overhead engineering and procurement support functions.

The design of GPM's very "customerized" movers will be a reversal from the current progression of design stages. Instead of setting the stylists to work on a clay model that is physically transported to engineers for process and material details, the process is reversed. Engineers "lay up" a base frame model on the screen, possibly downloaded from an optical scan of a life-size model; a separate but linked graphics system sits in the showroom. Production and tooling designs are then created in real-time linkage with concept design.

As engineering and production professionals begin to resemble each other more, supply managers will take on more of the functions just ahead of production: sourcing, quality, and some design functions. As a full member of the vehicle design team, procurement managers become experts at various component groups— seatbelts and seats, for example. Their training and experience is most likely in design and industrial engineering and they also understand the basics and advanced statistical quality control concepts, and are comfortable using them. Pricing is no problem;

as component group product managers, they have access to cost data and can get a reasonable fix on manufacturing and materials costs for each part managed in their data base. Base or target costs are on file, as are custom options.

GPM's commodity specialists work with supplier schedulers at GPM's showroom/factory to select the best range of custom options to meet GPM's target cost. The assumption is that all sourcing decisions fit the company's vision of high quality, competitive cost, and product availability.

Thus, what previously was a seatbelt procurement buying function and one of six thousand contributions to the finished product becomes a commodity expert job. The buyer now consults with customers when necessary, adjusts her assembly numbers accordingly, confers with suppliers, monitors quality performance stats, and runs target costs on a spreadsheet integrated into the company's unique CAD/CAM program, *Global Design*. Conversant in emerging technologies, the commodity sourcing expert understands what technologies are on the horizon, and plans new product transitions accordingly.

Finally, GPM's commodity expert is a superb communicator, equally comfortable standing at the blackboard and flipchart or seated at the design workstation. Her "people" skills are impressive: As a regular participant in supplier production meetings, her attendance is welcomed. Customers are not startled when her expert opinion is drawn into the specification discussions. Her résumé includes service on numerous design and network development teams.

It is, as the cinema cowboy said, "a tall order"—but not impossible. And certainly more fun than being the buyer for seatbelt, Part No. 01-49628, for thirty years or until retirement, whichever mercifully comes first.

FURTHER READING

For more on JIT see Shigeo Shingo, *A Study of the Toyota Production System* (Cambridge: Productivity Press, 1989), and Robert W. Hall, *Zero Inventories* (Homewood, Ill.: Business One Irwin, 1983).

For another vision of manufacturing futures, see Masuaki Iwata et al., *Manufacturing 21 Report: The Future of Japanese Manufacturing* (Wheeling, Ill.: Association for Manufacturing Excellence, 1990).

CHAPTER 3

New Organizational Structures— Building Blocks

*T*he obituary for the nearly successful job search could have read "He never knew what hit him." Ken Reeves, candidate for head of purchasing, had made it through four rounds of interviews with a large specialty chemicals producer. Lunch would wrap it up—the job offer would be made. . . . Over roast beef sandwiches and fries the conversation touched on the Red Sox—"Would they do it to us again this season?"—and the Celtics—"Would Larry Bird's knee injury cost the game with Atlanta?"—and "What are your feelings about going to lunch with vendors?"

Ken responded, "I don't go to lunch or dinner with vendors for three reasons: One, I don't have time; two, I don't want to put myself in a position that would compromise my ability to negotiate with vendors on behalf of my company; and three, quite honestly, because of the perception of purchasing, I don't want people internally talking it up."

It was all over. Although it is hard to fault that answer in some pockets of the purchasing world today, in the supply management community, where partnerships live and die on the strength of relationships, it was the *wrong* response. The client expressed disappointment: "The answer was old-fashioned, and set up an adversarial relationship with suppliers. We're interested in buyers who are going to work with our suppliers as partners and develop strong ties."

According to Robert McInturff, president of the firm that recruited the candidate, "Many people in industry still view the purchaser-vendor relationship with some trepidation. Ken could have said, 'I prefer not to go to lunch with suppliers to eliminate any appearance of impropriety. However, developing strong company-vendor relationships is important to me, and I've been able to get the same results by other means.' "

The company wanted to build partnerships with suppliers, not "keep vendors at bay." A bad question leading to a lousy answer. The focus became "Whom do you eat lunch with?" not "What should our relationship with our suppliers be?" Some members of the purchasing community see schmoozing as a reasonable component of a professional relationship. The client wanted a new-style manager, someone who could develop a partnership and not worry about lunch, a supply management professional who could form relationships.

The Touchpoints^{SM} of organization structure—where and with whom professionals work—and compensation and reward systems determine how well supply management organizations partner. When an organization is too complex, a maze of divided loyalties and responsibilities, or if valued personnel are not developed and rewarded for professional growth, the organization will not realize its full potential for outside partnering.

Further, organizations cannot ask their partners to exceed their own performance levels. Honda does not demand that its suppliers mirror its organization structure or training and development capabilities. Their suppliers are frequently smaller, older, focused on single processes or products. Honda's 30,000-employee global enterprise distributed over half a dozen plants is packed with a variety of processes and products that will not be replicated by most suppliers. The challenge is to understand, design, and build organization structures, work-force development, and compensation and reward systems that work best for partnership networks. Our focus in this chapter is organization structures and compensation and reward systems.

THREE ORGANIZATION BLOCKS

Three organization blocks must be in place to support development of the Seven Breakthrough Partnering Drivers.

The first organization block, *organization structure*, establishes linkages or touchpoints to support communications, the critical component of partnership development. Boeing's effective team structure—new product development teams, customer supplier teams, supplier teams—is typified by their agile design and rollout of the 777 twinjet faster than they dreamed possible following the 747 project's problems.

The second block, *people development*, supports personnel who are well positioned for partnership, enriching them with skills to stretch their own organizational capabilities. Honda, Motorola, and Xerox are pioneers in this area; smaller companies like Nypro and Seitz Corporation, a healthy Connecticut plastic supplier to Xerox and home to forty employees, are working to develop their human capital.

The third block, *compensation and reward systems*, cements the first two keystones. Without reinforcement and positive incentive to continue building trust between disparate individuals and groups, partnering falls back into the narrow confines of traditional bid-and-quote purchasing practices. Compensation is a critical success factor on two levels. First, individual contributors to purchasing, logistics, and other supply management functions should be compensated for creative work that places the company at the forefront of strong global sourcing. Second, supply managers should be compensated for developing the necessary expertise in a team environment. EMC Corporation's computer mass storage business requires intense attention to commodity and technology trends. Buyer-planners first of all know their commodities—where the technology is headed and when the next development will hit the market, and how to phase in new products over the old. Successful buyers become commodity experts. But if the company's senior commodity manager, Bill McGonagle, does not successfully take his product knowledge into the new product engineering arena, from which EMC introduces new products monthly, his skills are wasted.

ORGANIZATION STRUCTURE FOR ENTERPRISE INTEGRATION

An old Data General story illustrates how functional silos become barriers to internal partnering because the organization was not structured to foster good interdepartmental communications. Purchasing and materials personnel must broaden their scope to manage global sourcing strategy opportunities together.

Purchasing buyer Diane Brzezinski wanted to be the integrated circuits queen. It was a heady time at Data General in 1978 as bloodied competitors fought to keep a stranglehold on limited semiconductor memory production. Yields were uncertain— frequently entire lots turned bad at burn-in (the first time programmable chips were tested with power at receiving).

And yet Ellen Pinkham, the MRP planner who managed corporate memory requirements, and Brzezinski didn't talk. At opposite ends of the ring, each was poised to wrestle her opponent for dominance over this key commodity. And then, just outside their peripheral vision, something moved. Memory technology shifted from core, strings of magnetized metal "doughnuts" that were an expensive but predictable commodity filling the big appetites of mainframe customers, to semiconductor chips: cheap, small, and hot.

Both women missed it. Weekly shopping carts of "hernia reports," MRP printout runs, obscured the market shift. Unnoticed, customers continued to abandon room-size computers; orders for mini's flooded in. While Pinkham and Brzezinski struggled, the clock on the scoreboard ticked. By the time they fell back to their corners and Brzezinski declared herself the winner, it was too late. Core memory commitments were firm, and semiconductor supplies were well below customer demand. The new computer system introduction was doomed.

Internally, DG's career track was not designed to foster interdepartment cooperation in the materials world. Cubicles separated critical functions; computer printouts, overstuffed with forecast numbers, kept people busy. Decisions traveled up and down the hierarchy for a single powerful manager to handle, not a fast or informative communications structure in the exploding computer industry. Numbers wars flourished. The organization structure limited cross-functional contacts at great cost. Purchasing and material planning were segregated at all levels—from MIS system, through the management hierarchy. Career development was upward only. Cross-functional training was frowned upon in this stick-to-your-own business and upward-only career track.

Externally, the computer industry was a model of cutthroat competition among all parties, customers and suppliers alike. At Digital, even internal suppliers, like their Springfield, Massachusetts, cable assembly producers—located only 120 miles from the final assembly "customer" plant—might just as well have been on Mars. There were many cultural and professional differences between the two plants. Always out of synch, the Springfield facility was roughed up by periodic visits from the users, and whenever an opportunity to reciprocate arose, the Springfield plant took it. "Bad reps" spread: Springfield and a Boston plant were labeled "minority" suppliers by their customers.

Despite training and other good intentions, Digital's assorted plants never formed an integrated enterprise. And in fact, as the company faced downsizing, or "demassification," plants that were perceived as "different" or not part of the Digital culture were the first to be shut down. The Burlington, Vermont, facility, an island of innovation and enthusiasm insulated by distance from corporate daytrippers trying to manage by foray, was one of the first to be cut loose, a victim of its own strength. Had Digital eliminated politics and its focus on *superficial* diversity and created a few integrated enterprise groups, the resulting cuts would have better positioned the corporation to get back to business. A new personal computer enterprise organization map, anchored by Digital and outside software developers, might have looked like the arrangement in Figure 3.1.

Integrate for Enterprise Advantage

The challenge for big and small organizations is to realize the full potential of the integrated enterprise, an organic entity that easily flows, grows, and connects with other internal and external cells. The integrated enterprise is flexible, not constricted by rigid hierarchies and convoluted communications linkages. It is populated by supply management professionals who have the tools— electronic data transfer linkages, team mission statements, appropriate compensation, recognition and reward plans—to remove barriers that block integration of all the components required by a complete system. Financially, the customer and supplier organizations remain separate: The paper walls that define a corporate entity will still exist. Nevertheless, the vision of enterprise integration, of mutual interdependencies, is clear, epitomized by world-class examples such as Honda, Motorola, Solectron, and Nypro.

In the United States, Honda of America, Solectron, and Nypro have created the components of the integrated enterprise. In less than ten years Honda has developed a network of 246 suppliers to feed its assembly and engine plants, many of which are located within one day's drive of the customer's plant. Solectron's growth strategy positions new, customer-focused facilities in market

Figure 3.1: Integrated Personal Computer Enterprise

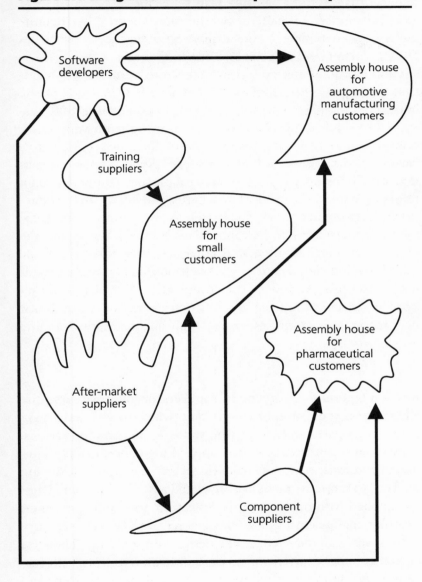

regions; that is, the California plants are not expected to serve global customers. Instead, the organization will grow by duplicating regional networks, by the acquisition of new facilities such as IBM's North Carolina plant and one in France.

CEO Gordon Lankton formulated Nypro's enterprise integration strategy as "the McDonald's approach to custom plastic injection molding." Nypro's network links Fortune 500 customers like J & J Vistakon, Gillette, and Verbatim with small, fast, and extremely high-quality ("CpK 2 or better," Nypro's version of Six Sigma) automated shops. Nypro chooses not to take on all customers. By focusing people and equipment on a few key partners, the product gets better and better, and production gets faster and faster. The better Nypro engineers and technicians understand J & J's contact lens business, the tighter the linkage will be. The integrated enterprise then takes the shape not of two individual entities, each responsible for separate products in the process flow to the end product, but of fully developed partners sharing the combined strengths of teams. Their new, integrated enterprises are fast, high-quality custom molding operations.

Alignment

Key to integrating customers and suppliers for collective enterprise advantage is the concept of alignment, which means developing parallel objectives and integration strategies in communications, systems, and cultures. Solectron applied the concept of the integrated enterprise to its core business several years ago. The driving goal was to keep customers like Hewlett-Packard, Apple, and Digital supplied with quality boards. Solectron now calls its business "turnkey manufacturing," working closely with customers to provide all value-added services like design and sourcing. The ideal customer-supplier arrangement for Solectron is to work with customers through a progression of product development, from planning through material acquisition, alpha build, and beta test, to full production. The supplier built a feeling of responsibility or "ownership," for the customer by involving planning people very early in the design cycle. This tactic guarantees better product because as Solectron's customers "design-in" recommended sources and components, production yields will be higher and costs lower.

Bob LeValley, manager of Solectron's East Coast business development, believes alignment is key to Solectron's successful partnerships and growth. To realize the potential of turnkey manufacturing, both partners need to stay in alignment, "take little steps, one step at a time, stay together. Keep checking to see everyone is still in agreement. Communications are extremely important in this business."

By structuring the engineering, order administration, and materials management systems with partitions between different customers' data to facilitate dealing with specific customer schedules and design issues, Solectron has assumed the customer's product and market identity. The symbiotic customer-supplier relationship has defined a new business for them both: the information business.

The U.S. auto industry faces the same integration challenge. The Big Three have yet to break the one-year concept-to-total-design barrier, but that is exactly what the new "people-moving" (auto) business must do. Detroit's design menu is a mix of clay, CAD/CAM and drafting, and Chrysler has successfully attempted faster "art-to-part" processes. Car design has traditionally moved from the vision of the designers to clay mock-ups transformed to tooling and computer simulations. Overlay a slide of the integrated enterprise on today's lengthy process, and the contrast illustrates complex linkages and numerous hand-offs. Within two years the systems integration and simulations tools, the missing links that stop organizations from completely reengineering their front-end processes, will be generally available to facilitate seamless "art-to-part" processes.

Beyond the traditional design boundaries, logistics departments, suppliers, and other functions from internal and external suppliers await integration. A direct approach to integration is new, simple organization structures.

Innovative Partnering Organizational Structures

In the 1980s, supply management organizations were called purchasing, or production control, or materials, or inventory control. All were responsible for using different tools and skill sets to accomplish essentially the same task: feeding production. The nomenclature reflected specific chunks of a complex process rendered even more complex by bringing materials through a centrally managed "push system." Material Requirements Planning, time-phased reorder point planning, even Economic Order Quantity calculations—all were driven from this top-down approach.

To the material planner, purchasing buyers seemed to command heavy negotiation skills. They traveled well and probably enjoyed the people side of the business more than the MRP-ers who managed with printouts and tended to have more MIS

FIGURE 3.2: Organizational Structures

DEGREE OF CROSS-FUNCTIONAL INTEGRATION

	Low cross-functional integration	High cross-functional integration
Buyer-planner	x	
Commodity manager	x	
Procurement teams		x
Subcontract administration specialists	x	
In-plants		x
Customer-supplier teams		x

involvement on their side of the cubicle. MRP-ers used communications and negotation skills too, but they also needed an analytical bent and the ability to express themselves day to day through numbers. The production planners who under the old approach were closest to "the heart of the beast"—shop operations— needed all the people and technical skills. Frequently cast in an intermediary role, they persuaded, explained, and threatened opposing constituencies into schedules that first of all met production goals, and second, satisfied customers.

This traditional organization structure is fragmented and contentious. Few planners or buyers are privileged to assemble all pieces of the material supply strategy into a coherent chain of events driven by a customer focus. The customer is located so far downstream that his or her voice is muted by all the intervening signals. Hand-offs cost time and money as the "functional silos" accumulate waste. And systems integration issues inevitably get in the way of daily operations flow.

These disjointed connections *can* be bridged. In supply management, as in many other institutions of the 1990s, pieces of the puzzle have already been recut. Organizations will continue to simplify and integrate systems expertise with product, customer, and process information. Functions previously cloistered in functional silos will have strange job titles, like New Product Purchasing/Engineering/Manufacturing Team Leader. The typical job descriptions will lengthen as the organization flattens and simplifies.

If simplification is the first crack in organizational barriers, getting closer to end customers and suppliers is the next. Several supply management organizations have drawn suppliers into their process; supplier personnel participate in customer quality and design, as well as price discussions. Bose Corporation, Boeing, EMC, and Apple Computer are examples of companies at the leading edge of this innovative organizational structure.

Bose Corporation

Bose Corporation of Framingham, Massachusetts, specialists in acoustical electronics, is continually challenged by successively more difficult quality and schedule demands by Japanese customers; one third of the company's revenues are from Japan. Tom Beeson, vice president of manufacturing, feels the organization has improved its ability to anticipate customer demands, and its flexibility, through its in-plant purchasing scheme, JIT II℠.

Lance Dixon, Bose's director of purchasing and logistics, has reached agreements with suppliers of plastics, printing, metal, transportation, packaging, resin, and customs brokerage to locate their representatives in-house. These people are called "in-plants." Suppliers for nonproprietary technologies obtain an evergreen contract in exchange for getting closer to this customer than ever before. These supplier personnel replace both the customer buyers and the supplier salespeople. Salaries are paid by the supplier, but the in-plant has complete access to the customer, from engineering meetings to the purchase order system and even to the receiving docks.

Chris LaBonte works for G & F Corporation in Stockbridge, one hour away from Bose's Westboro assembly plant. After spending an hour each morning at G & F, LaBonte, armed with a Bose badge, drives to Westboro for meetings with Bose production, purchasing, and engineering personnel. Together they plan and execute MRP and master schedules for G & F's plastic parts. Chris brings supplier plastics expertise in-house to Bose. He speeds materials planning and ordering by placing Bose *purchase orders directly on his own company.*

Bose also uses an in-plant for transportation. Transportation functions traditionally require a planner to contact carriers and schedule shipments; multiple sources are used, ranked by cost. Bose's logistics functions cover a reduced number of carriers. EDI

(Electronic Data Interchange) has augmented the company's JIT capabilities to partner with logistics suppliers and the company also automates bill of lading creation and on-line shipment status. By partnering with W. I. Proctor, freight forwarders and customs brokers, Bose has located a licensed customers broker in-house to facilitate international traffic. The broker works as an in-plant with access to on-line shipping information and can track and speed release of inbound freight. Any customer that has attempted to clear priority shipments through slow ports appreciates the wisdom of having an expert in house who can move material and redirect shipments to avoid bottlenecks.

In-plants offer Bose a range of benefits:

■ In-plants have access to new product design programs and can, with their expertise, influence the design process.

■ Bose offers its suppliers an added incentive to discover product/process improvements. Through value analysis on the existing product base, suppliers keep one-half of the savings on cost reductions they create—forever. For example, when one supplier recommended that Bose change a speaker grill from aluminum to steel, thereby changing the finishing material as well, the cost dropped 20 percent, half of which went to the supplier.

■ Bose's vendor engineering function resides in the procurement organization, so purchasing can assist suppliers, helping, say, G & F Corporation reach high quality levels in plastic injection molding, through better process control.

■ When Bose introduces new products in Massachusetts, prototypes developed in Boston eventually move on to a satellite plant. Typically, a satellite start-up would bring in new suppliers at the bottom of the learning curve. Under JIT II, some in-plants travel to the satellite to assist in the process. G & F's in-plant is helping satellite plants to start production on new products that have already been produced in Massachusetts. Participating in both start-ups eliminates frantic "your parts don't work" phone calls because LaBonte has identified problems to the new plant in advance.

At the suggestion of Bose management, G & F purchased a new plant in Ireland, located close to Bose's new facility, a move designed to give both companies better access to the Common Market. G & F can move a proven tool supporting Massachusetts production to the Irish plant, thereby accelerating the start-up.

Although the initial focus of in-plant purchasing started with supplier reps, Bose now sends engineers out to its partners. Steve Parker, whose regular assignment was plastic tooling procurement, spent three months with Bose's plastics supplier. His assignment? To review each part for process and design opportunities, tooling, and equipment selection.

The initial impetus for Bose's partnering arrangement was fiscal constraints. Growth in the usual salesperson/buyer/planner structure gets expensive. Bose's volume and parts lists were growing, but head counts could not. The supplier's in-house representative is not a salesperson—that function is eliminated in this arrangement. The cost of maintaining a full-time professional at the customer's plant may be more than the cost of a salesperson servicing several accounts, but additional costs are offset by the supplier's single-source status.

As the single supplier expert for that commodity group, the in-plant speaks for the supplier on diverse issues: production schedules, costs, quality, transportation, technical advances. As an adviser to Bose designers, the in-plant helps design products "a better way," with better materials that incorporate design for manufacturability and time-to-market solutions.

For the customer, this arrangement frees up professionals from a heavy paperwork processing load and tracking and expediting. It also allows a group to develop and reward commodity experts, or commodity teams who do long-range planning and sourcing, then execute the sourcing strategy. Other benefits include the following: Communications between customer and supplier are streamlined, effectively based on two people rather than four. Plant visits are replaced with in-house assists. Quality issues specific to supplier materials become clearer sooner. One in-plant supplier, a speaker box producer, learned what Bose meant by "cosmetic integrity," i.e., a perfect paint job, when the customer helped build a $100,000 paint room within sixty days from the start of discussions.

Partners with Bose must demonstrate "best-in-class" performance and consistently good quality, delivery, and cost. The supplier must also offer engineering support. Selection criteria include:

- Dollar volume in excess of one million
- Substantial number of purchase order transactions
- "Evolving" technology
- Confidentiality issues regarding supplier's trade secrets or sensitive technology

The Bose in-plants are a powerful assemblage of procurement and product/process talent. With planning and scheduling tasks added to the job description, it makes sense that they make more money and decisions than traditional buyers/planners. Bose operates in a leaner, flatter organization than before, because the in-plant system allows them to acquire information, usually first hand, at higher operating levels.

Apple Computer

Apple's supply management group has always been lean. Now, with new computer product introductions accelerating at increasing speeds, the company has reinvented its approach to partnering with suppliers. Apple purchasing pros are commodity specialists with expertise in price, available and emergent technologies, and new product requirements. In addition, the company has opened its doors to supplier representatives for some commodities, much like Bose's JIT II scheme.

Commodity specialists are frequently out of the shop, and the company has also recently substituted some videoconferencing for travel. Supply managers focus their procurement and tracking work around the MAP, the Materials Acquisition Plan. A strategic long-term and tactical short-term operating guide, MAP serves as a summary of procurement plans. Ninety percent of the cost of goods sold is purchased materials; the MAP is key to managing that figure.

Apple positions high-level combined purchasing and engineering expertise with the MAP, to place supply management ahead of the rest of the organization. The MAP horizon is five years, with updates every two or three months, or as required. The document includes supplier selection criteria, and quality, delivery and pricing information. It should identify potential problems in advance of production. Organized into commodity groups—for example, memories and power supplies—each MAP contains five sections, including an overview on industry trends, capacity, and pricing data.

EMC Corporation

EMC Corporation, another young enterprise, of Hopkinton, Massachusetts, has redesigned its traditional purchasing department. A producer of mass storage systems, EMC decided to speed its growth with big inventory reductions, but to do this the company had to look beyond typical JIT approaches. A unique organization solution came from buyer Judy Lazaros, who felt that the buyer/planners needed to get out of the day-to-day tactical material movement game and shift some of that responsibility to the suppliers of components.

Judy worked out an arrangement with distributors Anthem and

Hallmark, both located twenty miles away, to take over ordering and replenishment. Four distributor representatives signed up: Two visit once per week, and two "live" at EMC. They access both the EMC and their home MRP systems. Starting with the EMC MRP run, including the forecast, they calculate an on-shelf quantity, "suggested" to be three months usage, which they maintain for the customer offsite. The in-plants have limited access to the system. They enter paperless purchase orders and review them, including ship dates and quantities or prices.

EMC in-plants carry contract badges, pay their own phone bills, and sign in and out. Unlike the Bose in-plants they do not access engineering. The arrangement is verbal, not written, and like all true partnerships, it benefits both sides. EMC takes a big cut out of inventory, amounting to about $2 million in savings.

The results of this simplification of the supply pipeline earned Ms. Lazaros an MVP (Most Valuable Person) Award. Hard-copy purchase orders and change-orders were eliminated, at a savings of $110 per event. Other benefits accrue to the customer: The minimum dollar order is small, and with smaller lot sizes, inventory turns faster. The order window for cancellations and reschedules dropped to two days. Lead time dropped from six weeks to three days, a strategic requirement for EMC's very competitive business. On-time delivery soared to 100 percent, and distributors have agreed to drop-ship directly to EMC's Puerto Rico plant, thereby eliminating kitting time and expenses at the Hopkinton plant. The company recognizes that focusing business with fewer distributors is better than managing ten or more.

Boeing

Innovative supply management structures are equally important in big, more mature organizations like Boeing, where customer-supplier teams have been created.

Boeing's latest development program, the 777 twinjet, designed to move wide-body-sized passsenger loads over long routes, is an innovation both technologically and in its team design process. According to John Roundhill, who served as 777 chief project engineer, one of the objectives of the team has been to make the jet service-ready for quick turnarounds. "We are working very hard with customers," he says, "approaching the design in more depth, early in the program." Four of Boeing's big 777 customers, United, ANA (All Nippon Airways), British Airways, and Japan Airlines, are working onsite with Boeing engineers on the detail design.

The customer-supplier collaboration concept was born in October 1990, when the 777 project was formally launched. Roundhill calls it "a great idea . . . very simple."

Customer team members work full time with the supplier in their engineering group. The aircraft operator representatives bring customer insight to the design process regarding attention to maintenance, reliability, and other postsales customer issues.

The direct involvement of the customer airlines in 777 development is a logical consequence of Boeing's market-driven approach to sizing the aircraft prelaunch. United, ANA, British Airways, and JAL were among a number of carriers with whom Boeing held substantive discussions, including many group sessions, to define the aircraft's design. Gordon McKinzie, United's 777 program manager, contrasts this new collaboration with the old days, when "we'd order the airplane, write letters back and forth, and then five years later pick [it] up."

How has early customer involvement changed the process and design of the 777 for Boeing and its partners? Better repair technology and lower costs, with faster turnarounds, are on the punch list. For example, the 777 large outboard trailing edge, which is one of the aircraft's longest pieces and holds trailing edge flaps made of composites, presented a problem: Sometimes the edges are hit by stones and damaged during takeoff. Airlines often repair composites in autoclaves, but because this section is 45 feet long, it can't be easily transported. Solution: The design team suggested splitting the member into two parts.

The location of the electronics bay access hatch, another "customer" issue, was changed to accommodate safety. Early in the design process, customer team members pointed out that they had had numerous accidents when maintenance personnel pulled off the hatch door to perform maintenance, forgot about the hole, and fell in. If the door were located on the same side as the galley door, turnaround time would drop. And since airlines need speedy turnarounds, they would like to service the galley and electronics at the same time.

The team's solution was to put the hatch on the side where passengers enter, as far forward as possible. ANA suggested a design modification of adding a hinge with an automatic closure to the hatch so that when the mechanic enters, the hinge closes the door.

An infinite number of innovative partnering arrangements are possible—organizations and people are the only limitations. What makes very simple partnering initiatives work with companies like Bose, EMC, and Boeing is an organization that recognizes the synergy possible from combining forces, and a reward and recognition system that smiles on individuals as they step out of the traditional purchasing approach to team with customers and suppliers.

A Negative Example

A New York producer of temperature controls and sensors illustrates how *not* to start an internal restructuring process. The purchasing organization was populated with traditional buyers and supervisors directed by a purchasing manager, located in comfortable, well-furnished corporate offices far from the action. The company president sought to make big white-collar process changes by radically redesigning the purchasing department's activities. Although his specific objectives were unclear, the hope was that throwing out the traditional structure would somehow bring inventories down and improve parts quality.

First, all purchasing personnel were ordered to move out to the production floor, next to parts bins and within calling distance of the assemblers. No room here for confidential discussions with suppliers; price and contractual meetings suddenly took place "in the open."

The next step was to combine master scheduling and material requirements planning tasks with purchasing order placement and tracking. All materials and planning functions were moved into the same physical space, immediately next to assembly and bin storage area. Purchasing, materials, and scheduling each still reported to different managers. It was a strange arrangement. Although master scheduling and material buyer-planners were physically closer, communications did not improve.

The next step hurt morale. The purchasing department lost one clerk and a buyer; the purchasing manager was demoted to buyer, reporting to a vice president of quality, who now "owned" purchasing, MRP, and master scheduling. Paperwork did not go away, so the survivors' work load increased. On a plant visit one day after the "no suits/no ties" rules took effect, an outsider heard much grumbling: There was little privacy, there were no quiet areas for thinking, a process that any organization in this business would need. Buyers who had worked for fifteen years in shirts and ties, for whom a sportcoat and corner office meant they had "made it," found themselves without milestones. The move had accomplished its purpose—to flatten the old hierarchy—but without explanations and new rewards, the group was in chaos.

Buyers knew they no longer constituted a purchasing department, but they had no clues about what they were becoming. How much more effective the transition would have been had the president shared his vision of supply management and the new partnerships he hoped to create!

Restructuring a traditional purchasing organization into teams can't be made to work well simply because the lines are redrawn on paper. Teams don't develop overnight.

WHAT'S SO SPECIAL ABOUT TEAMS?

As we grow up, we participate in teams. If we don't play football or basketball, we participate in choir (musical teams) or study groups and Boy Scouts. Teams are not new, but this doesn't mean that effective teams are easy to achieve. As the vice president of operations at a Midwest engine assembler said, "I don't get it. Teams are so simple. Why can't we do it?"

Teams are an essential part of enterprise integration because internal project teams draw on the flexibility and talent of individuals. Group decisions should be better than those made by individuals—"Two heads are better than one." Like the commodity teams at Apple, groups of experts are better able to keep up with technology trends while they "mind the store."

Traditional organizations get into trouble with what Colorado compensation expert Alan Siebenaler calls the "megaphone and pom-pom" approach to teams. The creation of effective teams requires more than corporate cheerleading. The problem is that hierarchies cannot find a place for team structures somewhere on their organization chart. When companies attempt to form teams without changing the reporting structures and internal communications linkages, thereby weakening the hierarchy, or if the compensation system fails to recognize team performance, the team becomes a resource pool that still takes direction from higher management levels. It is not truly self-directed. The net result is the impression that teams are "just another way to get more out of us."

Traditional purchasing organizations have more difficulty keeping teams going than new companies in the initial start-up phase. Supply management is a dynamic, growing area, filled with excitement and challenges. Professionals are not drawn to this function unless they have a high tolerance for pressure and balancing competing objectives, all issues that teams encounter early on. But compensation systems must reward commodity specialists for meeting long-term and partnering goals. If the system rewards only buyers who hammer purchase price variances to cut supplier costs, the reward structure undermines the intent of internal and external partnership efforts.

COMPENSATION

Compensation and reward systems are the power that places the organization behind the people. Compensation and rewards are not always monetary. In fact, few companies have deep pockets these days—not large corporations, and certainly not small ones. Creatively attracting and rewarding supply management talent is a challenge facing all companies. As a result, organizations have developed powerful nonmonetary rewards that have proved effective in satisfying employees' need to be recognized as valued contributors.

A materials disaster at a Midwest communications systems manufacturer was turned around by a buyer's after-hours dedication. A shipment of custom prototype boards arrived with the circuit layout, the component footprint was reversed. Friday evening, the buyer reached the president of the board manufacturer at home, and the executive agreed to bring in a weekend crew. The buyer then coordinated an express delivery of revised drawings to the plant, and on Monday, the reworks arrived, ready for insertion. Thanks to the buyer's diligence, the customer's order was shipped on time.

As a thank-you, the buyer received a merit award and a bonus of 3 percent of her base pay. She was also authorized to thank her suppliers by ordering a catered lunch for the Saturday crew, thereby strengthening her customer-supplier partnership.

EMC Corporation announces one MVP award per department each month to recognize individual performance. One recipient had set up an offsite workshop that was conducted without a hitch. Her name was added to a bronze plaque in the entrance lobby for a year, and she received a $100 cash bonus, as well as a preferred parking spot in the garage next to the door for one month. Another EMC employee was praised by her internal customers for being especially helpful. The worker later got a visit from the company's vice president, Michael Schoonover, who awarded her a chit for dinner and babysitting.

But individual awards alone do not build group spirit, and group recognition is also important. One simple but effective method of rewarding a group and promoting enthusiasm was demonstrated by a New Hampshire manager who showed up unannounced at a team meeting and distributed $25 certificates to a local supermarket to each team member.

Another Midwestern company is experimenting with gift catalogs as part of its reward system. Participants in engineering, purchasing, quality, and production can earn points as they participate in various team tasks. As they accumulate points, the team members cash the points in for tape players, dinners, or event tickets. They can even save them for large prizes such as cruises and airplane tickets. All the awards are substantial, because the company is aware that rapid and smooth new product introductions gain market and make money, and it believes the rewards should be commensurate with the gain.

Perhaps this electronic assembler's most creative compensation scheme is the King/Queen for a Day award, which goes to the individual who makes the largest contribution to cost reductions. In recognition of the worker's accomplishments, the company gives the employee a couple of days off with free use of a company car (the vice president's Cadillac!), plus enough cash to fill the tank. Immediacy is important. When purchasing managers here notice anyone from purchasing, procurement engineering, or the support staff who deserves recognition, the employee becomes eligible for an Instant Award—a weekend package for two at a nearby resort hotel.

One Friday night, a manager called in and found a clerical support person still working, trying to catch up on her computer work. If she didn't get the requisitions in, there would be chaos Monday morning, the clerk explained. Although data input was her job, working after eight was beyond normal expectations. She was immediately given an Instant Award.

Gainsharing Systems

Most compensation systems periodically review and reward *individual* contributions. Because few pay structures deal with teams, rewarding cooperative team efforts is a challenge.

A compensation scheme that is gaining adherents is gainsharing, which is simply a group incentive plan or pay for performance, under which employees as a group earn bonuses for cooperating to improve plant performance. Gainsharing plans draw on the best ideas and suggestions of the participants to capitalize on productivity and quality improvements. They can be used on top of regular wage structures to reward employees for performance "above and beyond" and for cooperative efforts that require great investment in time for team meetings and other cross-functional activities, like participation in commodity teams, new product introduction teams, or customer/supplier project teams.

Chicago consultant Woodruff Imberman estimates that there are over two thousand gainsharing plans in existence, mainly among manufacturers, but also in many service enterprises like banks, hospitals, insurance companies, and nonprofits and not-for-profits. They can be designed not just to reward increased shipments or cost reduction. According to Imberman, gainsharing plans have been installed in "white-collar factories" of banks and insurance companies to reward employees if errors in loan applications or insurance policy changes are reduced. Any organization in which employee efforts can be measured can improve its performance through the installation of a gainsharing plan. Certainly in supply management, where teams are formed to speed new product introductions or to improve supplier relations (improved quality and flexibility), measurements related to specific objectives should form the basis of group reward schemes.

When gainsharing plans link support personnel from purchasing and materials management with production, they improve the consistency of focus on the business's strategic objectives. The incentive plan becomes another barrier breaker, a force that integrates functions on both sides of the factory wall.

THE VALUE OF RECOGNITION

Dave King, purchasing administrator at Honda, was assigned the task of increasing locally sourced content for cars assembled at the Ohio plant. Honda had already undergone a push to locally source its 1986, 1987, and 1988 models.

A typical bill of materials for a car lists around 6,000 parts. Earlier, the localization focus had been on big-dollar items that were the most costly to ship. But in December 1991 it accelerated this strategy by specifying a dollar amount of parts to be bought locally. This "voluntary plan," as Honda calls it, states that the company will manufacture where it sells, and buy where it manufactures.

The voluntary plan has shifted attention toward the smaller and more technology-driven parts. Parts are reviewed by 17-member voluntary teams, made up of representatives from purchasing, supplier development, parts quality, and Honda Research of America. After a strategy is planned and confirmed by manufacturing, purchasing begins sourcing.

King implemented a unique method of increasing domestic purchases. He parked a large trailer outside the purchasing department and loaded it with the 1,500 auto parts that Honda purchased from Japanese sources. He directed his buyers to go in, pull out a part, and find a U.S. source for it. His goal was to empty the trailer.

"We had already increased local content to approximately 75 percent [the Environmental Protection Agency's formula for all automakers]," said King. The EPA formula takes into account not only parts and materials, but also labor, marketing, and other administrative costs.

The parts in King's trailer are color-coded: A green dot means the part will be localized by fiscal year 1995; yellow indicates further investigation is needed; and red means the part cannot be localized in the near future. "By looking at the tags," King notes, "buyers can see what they will be working on for the next three years."

Such an important program idea is not rewarded with money. According to King, a real incentive for this level participation is the opportunity to make a presentation to Honda's president, to have his own ideas respected and valued, and to know that his color-coded solution is very important to Honda's future.

Honda recognizes other partners for their participation. In April, suppliers visit the plant for a day of recognition. Also in April, supplier and other interested partners participate in a Honda Benchmarking Conference, where ideas and objectives are traded, along with stories about what worked and what didn't. Inclusion in this group of thought leaders is a reward in itself.

FOUR POINTS FOR ORGANIZATIONAL CHANGE

Supply management partners in the integrated enterprise need to focus on four issues:

1. Technical expertise
2. Organizational structure
3. Communications
4. Recognition and reward systems

Technical expertise, knowing where the absolute best suppliers are located, and how technology trends impact new product plans, continues to be the responsibility of supply management professionals. In their supplier development toolkit they pack statistical process control, along with well-developed people and team skills. When the organization's three blocks are in place— streamlined horizontal structure, an attitude that fosters workforce professional development, and compensation and reward systems—the organization stands behind the individual. Without backing on these three fronts, individual partnership initiatives will at some point in the development of the alliance, fail.

FURTHER READING

For more on compensation systems, see Scott Myers, *Every Employee a Manager* (San Diego: Pfeiffer, 1991). This book includes wonderful case histories of unusual compensation schemes.

See also Donna Neusch and Alan F. Siebenaler, *The High Performance Enterprise* (Essex Junction, Vt.: Oliver Wight Publications, 1993).

CHAPTER 4

Benchmarking the Best

The room was filled with assorted consultants and information system experts, all shuffling impatiently through their findings. The group was ready to decide whose manufacturing planning software package would be chosen for implementation at eighteen sites. The winner's revenues would jump by several million dollars. Since installation for the beta site would probably take eight to twelve months, the group was eager to start.

Analysis and recommendations began. For three weeks two software packages had been put through their paces as the software gurus tested the program's technical abilities: speed, capacity for processing massive data transactions, recovery and compilation times. They called it exercising the system, or benchmarking. (*Benchmarking*, quite simply, is the *systematic* investigation of the capabilities of other organizations, in order to develop improvement targets.)

The results pointed overwhelmingly to a complex seven-year-old software package priced at $175,000 whose heart, a bill of material processor (BOM), had demonstrated great capacity for processing complex assemblies in record time. But wait! The application was order administration in warehouses and distribution centers, neither of which really needed a bill of material processor, the meatgrinder that breaks top-level assembly requirements into their smallest components, offsetting the subassemblies and units in weekly time buckets. Warehouses and distribution centers process thousands of receiving and shipping transaction reports, so inventory maintenance and audit trails are important. The package had no backlog customer order detail and no distribution network pegging. Hmm . . . Was this truly benchmarking? Could they have skipped a step or two?

Fifteen years ago this *was* benchmarking, i.e., testing the technical abilities of a software package. The original idea was to push a system through various transaction processing loads, looking for breaking points and tangled audit trails. The final decision was in the hands of the systems gurus.

THE PROMISE OF BENCHMARKING

> I think people here expect miracles. American management thinks that they can just copy from Japan. But they don't know what to copy.
>
> *J. Edwards Deming, quoted by Mary Walton in* The Deming Management Method

Unfortunately, the current definition and purpose of benchmarking is still unclear, despite much activity and a plethora of seminars. Benchmarking as a hot trend has been recrafted, has peaked, and is beginning to lose its magic as the first wave of benchmarkers wear out their welcome with world-class companies. Initial benchmarking efforts frequently amount to junkets because team members have little to offer in return for the information on processes secured from their host. Like the system specification steps in the software award story, primary research (looking at internal operations) and secondary research (literature and database searches) are often missing.

The problem is not the concept; it's the execution. Benchmarking, looking at world-class examples of best practice and comparing them to one's own operation, is a marvelous tool that takes a team beyond its own boundaries. It is an essential tool for companies looking to improve their internal partnering abilities. Each of the Seven Breakthrough Partnering Drivers—quality, timeliness, excellent communications, flexibility, the attitude of continuous improvement, collaboration, and trust—are further strengthened by customer-supplier partners who benchmark and take action to ratchet up their organization's performance.

According to Dave Curry of Honda of America, no benchmarking drive is worth the effort without the commitment to follow up on improvement opportunities. For customer-supplier teams, benchmarking is a continuous improvement aid. Greg Watson, Xerox's vice president of total quality, defines benchmarking as "a business tool for helping to understand and anticipate the potential moves of competitors . . . a structured approach to gaining information that will help your organization anticipate the whitewater and improve its ability to steer through the business environment."[1]

Most customer and supplier benchmarkers are interested in a few key functions that will determine how well they actually partner. Supply management performance in specific functional areas—e.g., planning, buying, and commodity teams—and communications are the immediate targets. Other functional areas such as logistics and accounts payable come into play because they also impact a customer's or supplier's ability to partner.

One supply management benchmarking team organized its project around benchmarking processes for the following five topics:

1. Payment terms
2. Commodity–product manager organization, including sub-contract administration. This category covered questions on

   - purchasing headcount
   - sales dollars per buyer/planner
   - total dollars spent with suppliers
   - salaries and benefits as a percent of the purchasing budget

- active suppliers
- number of meetings with suppliers attended by average buyer
- buyer/planner education and training levels
- percent of transactions performed electronically
- time to place or respond to order
- amount of time spent benchmarking
- use of customer-supplier scorecard.

3. Supplier rating, certification, development and recognition systems
4. Cross training, commodity exchange
5. Reduction of non-value-added purchasing activities.

Each of the Seven Drivers can also be benchmarked—including the seventh driver, trust. But it is the most difficult to quantify because it is a desired outcome of perfecting the other six partnership drivers.

The challenge for benchmarkers is to identify the *right* measure and to locate a company to serve as an excellence model. The model company must be willing to share its quantitative performance measurements, as well as operating details that show how it reached its current performance level.

BENCHMARKING THE BREAKTHROUGH PARTNERING DRIVERS

1. *Quality*

Benchmarking is a quality tool mentioned in at least twelve of the thirty-plus criteria for the Baldrige Award. Quality, the first driver, translates in a variety of ways in different industries with unique measures of excellence. As a result, the benchmarks will vary. In the electronics sector, process controls and other proofs of an organization's ability to control and correct for quality problems are more important than a simple reading of the product defect levels—errors per million parts, for example. Would-be bench-markers, therefore, need a clear definition of what they hope to learn that will support their own strategic objectives.

In the software benchmarking story, team members skipped from the definition of strategic objectives to tactical details—*how* the system operated, rather than *what* it did. Had they defined strategic objectives first, they would have identified a quality problem in the warehouse: orders missing line items, forgotten back orders, missing paperwork—all problems that could have been resolved with operating changes, not a multi-million-dollar MRP package! First they would have defined their customer's *acceptable* service level. Their strategic objective, therefore, might have been to fill all customer orders from the warehouse in forty-eight hours or less with no errors or back orders. Next, they would have identified an excellence model, like L. L. Bean, whose success is dependent on superb order filling. Finally, their benchmarking partnering project would have taken them inside L. L. Bean to observe the company's real-time distribution system.

2. Timeliness

Federal Express and Walmart base all their processes on timeli-ness. The success of their approach is measured in growth and retention of market share. In thirty years, Walmart has grown from nine stores ringing up $1.4 million sales to 1,528 stores totaling $26 billion in sales in 1990, according to Sam Walton's biography *Made in America: My Story.*

The best way to identify time opportunities is for bench-markers to do a simple flowchart, or a process flow, of their operations, including at each step of the way the time required to perform the task, the number of steps involved, and the names of the processors. The straightforward exercise of following a cus-tomer order through convoluted order administration, material planning, and production cycles uncovers surprises. You will see not only that there are "dead spots," areas where paperwork sits or is detoured off the main traffic flow, but that the sum of the process is often greater than the parts. The process reveals how an operation actually integrates its separate functions.

The experience of a Midwest automotive subassembly manufacturer illustrates this point. As the company was considering slight modifications to their material planning system, one team member took a radically different approach to what was generally perceived as an inventory problem. He mapped the entire planning cycle on a six-foot-long flow chart, with dotted lines indicating where paperwork crossed an invisible departmental line. The exercise of constructing "the map" was a good "weight control" exercise because the examiner walked several miles, from cubicle to cubicle, asking the same questions of various participants: "What is this paper? Where does it go from here?"

The final conclusion was that this organization had structured its planning functions around a pre–World War II vision of planning intended to drive massive batches of material down long assembly lines. Huge chunks of data were moved, thrown, nudged, and dragged along until they reached purchasing— where the next data chunk was ready to drop into the hopper. Everything happened serially, nothing was in parallel. Quite a discovery! Tweaking the system or adding a few more planners en route would not fix a basically flawed process flow. *It had to be redesigned for speed.*

3. Communications

To customer-supplier partners, communications are either frequent and clear, or useless. Some typical indicators of good communications are subjective. The following checklist represents a good starting point for benchmarking a supply management organization's communications activities:

- Percent of buyer/planner time spent with suppliers and/or customers
- Use of electronic communications aids: EDI linkages for schedules, MRP requirements, and the frequency of their transmission
- Time required to respond to immediate concerns
- Maintenance by customer/supplier partner of a single contact point (your own "service representative") committed to rapid response
- Personnel who are trained and comfortable with group presentation skills
- Feedback structure: customer-conducted regular feedback surveys, customer-sponsored onsite periodic supplier days, existence of an active supplier council

4. Flexibility

For customers, flexibility is usually a code word for scheduling flexibility: the ability of suppliers to quickly change product ship dates, quantities, or specifications. For suppliers, flexibility means the hoped-for flexibility of customers whose systems can accommodate last-minute deviations from schedule or ship quantity. Of course, JIT is also very important to customers who run lean production operations, as GM discovered when a strike at Lordstown, Ohio, almost shut down the Saturn assembly plant. Flexibility may not reside at the actual customer or supplier partner's site, but in the pipeline where skilled logistics linkages bend to accommodate schedule changes.

Measuring flexibility is not as difficult as it might seem. If schedule flexibility is the strategic issue, the measure of that element is a supplier's adherence to a schedule and its ability to absorb customer requests for differing ship dates and quantities. Shorter leadtimes may not indicate that a supplier is supremely flexible, but getting a critical part two weeks before your competitor is adequate flexibility in the marketplace. Process flexibility may mean that a plastics supplier has the capital equipment in place to move a customer's design to a higher-quality or higher-speed machine.

Benchmarking teams can evaluate flexibility in two basic ways:

- Objectively, through quantitative measures
- Subjectively, through evaluations by key customers of a supplier's ability to respond to new product challenges

5. The Attitude of Continuous Improvement

Ken Stork, former Motorola director of purchasing and materials, feels strongly about the correct use of benchmarking—"Time Out! We need a new law; no one may utter the word 'benchmarking' until they have completed the following:

1. No one may accept or delegate authority to begin a benchmarking study without a clear understanding of its purpose, desired objectives, etc.

2. No new questionnaire may leave your company without providing the potential benchmarking hosts your internal status/responses to your own questions.

3. Peer-to-peer benchmarking exchanges only. No more "employees you can spare" sent to visit CEOs. Your CEO needs to do it, too.

4. Any benchmarker who, after completing the team's benchmarking report, fails to lead dramatic change in his organization will be fired and lose all pension and social security benefits."[2]

Companies like Motorola and Sun Microsystems use benchmarking as a major contributor to their continuous improvement strategies. In supply management, the benchmarking challenge is not necessarily the process—books by Michael Spendolini,

Robert Camp, and Greg Watson will all get you started *if* you have identified the areas that need improvement. Sun's Peggy Williams recommends that in supply management an organization must pick the right improvement targets *first*: "Traditional purchasing practice reinforces narrow purchasing activities that foster leveraged, cost-only relationships. When the measures change, behavior follows."

Steve Kelley, manager of advanced manufacturing technology for Sun's Chelmsford, Massachusetts, plant, recently led a unique benchmarking project. The company set out to identify how Sun's product reliability, usually measured as Mean Time Between Failure (MTBF) or Mean Time Between Repair (MTBR), compared with that of the competition, a more difficult research job than benchmarking against best practice models because the data is more difficult to uncover. Four major competitors were selected. "When you talk about reliability," says Kelley, "everybody has a different definition; it's really customer *perception*. The challenge was to do a comparison and use some kind of scale. Because most of the data is not published, we couldn't get performance stats on standard tests undergone by each competitor."

The team chose to develop one methodology to compare all four competitors. The emphasis was on developing standard, repeatable measurements rather than a perfect quantitative assessment. Kelley felt that if the project yielded information on current product reliability, it would be easy to compare the next generation's percent improvement down the road. So the assessments looked at the product two ways: compared to the competition, and compared to earlier generations of Sun product.

Understanding the perception of reliability is where benchmark evaluations turn from quantitative to subjective, says Kelley. "Sony, for example, creates the perception of quality and reliability for which customers will pay slightly more. Panasonic's name might evoke a different reaction, but if we broke the two brands' products down, we would probably not find much variation except in perception." Customer perception of reliability is built up in a number of ways, not just through the measurable hardware performance. Service, packaging, availability, and image are all contributors.

Kelley's experience with a previous benchmarking exercise was markedly different. The earlier exercise took approximately six months to complete, whereas this one, which he describes as a "very focused project," was designed, like Sun's product cycle itself, for quick completion in about one and a half months.

A Hewlett-Packard team, eager to benchmark their semiconductor performance against internal and external competitors, threw a "wild party" to kick off their benchmarking efforts. Team members gathered for several hours of pizza and literature searches, their first step before database reviews. Trips, according to team co-leader Lucy Crespo, were absolutely the last step. As the entire benchmarking process becomes a data-gathering exercise with increased team involvement the group will continually improve its benchmarking skills.

6. The Habit of Collaboration

Benchmarking an organization's ability and practice of collaboration is extremely subjective. Ask partners about the number of teams they have served on in the past year, and have them identify their current team assignments. At one East Coast electromechanical controls producer, most purchasing and manufacturing personnel have served on five or six teams in two years. Other indicators of strong commitment include collaborations with various professional groups, or, especially important for small companies, pooling resources with others for training.

The second major contributor to effective collaboration is reward systems. When personnel are expected to participate in cross-functional teams, they should be rewarded for their work. A medical devices manufacturer is experimenting with a catalog reward system that allows personnel to accumulate prizes chosen from a catalog, including time off and resort trips, in recognition of cross-functional project work.

Protocol

All good collaborations are bounded by rules of conduct, or protocol. Protocol is the way meetings are conducted, and may be covered by written collaboration agreements which reveal much about a group's approach. When a potential partner initiates linkage without a protocol—introductions, collaboration agreements, and agendas—the best intentions can be undermined by secondary agendas and daily emergencies.

In any partnering activity, especially benchmarking, protocol makes or breaks the success of the project. Writing down the rules in advance keeps secondary agendas in control and gives participants the freedom to make the most of the exercise without concerns over information leaks. A typical benchmarking team will set rules governing the following five areas:

1. "Housekeeping:" e.g., escort requirements, meeting location, notes.
2. Confidentiality rules: e.g., "No sensitive information," "All discussion is for the record."
3. Objectives: e.g., "to bring people together to discover ideas that can be further developed in one-on-one sessions," "to produce a written report for the partner," "to continue the process with educational events and public forums."
4. Agenda: agreed on and published in advance; includes role of facilitators, meeting feedback checklist."
5. Participation: Participants decide when and to whom to open

the group, and whether to make available attendee names and phone/fax listings. Finally, the group may set minimum attendance rules, or some other mechanism to guarantee ongoing commitment to the process.

Of these five points, confidentiality is especially important because it explains why, although the process of benchmarking is a hot topic, detailed results are difficult to share. The shadow of industrial espionage hangs over many intercompany contacts. Had the British prevented Francis Cabot Lowell from visiting their cotton mills in 1812 and memorizing the design of their power looms, they would not have lost dominance of that industry to the United States. Two brilliant individuals, Lowell and industrial engineer Paul Moody, were all it took for the mill city of Lowell to seize the British stand-alone textile production concept and integrate the entire production process that dominated world markets for the next 150 years.

INDUSTRY BENCHMARKS

Sun Microsystems, Inc.

Peggy Williams, director of supply management for Sun Microsystems in California, takes a very simple approach to benchmarking. She participated in and guided a benchmarking study undertaken by seventy-five Silicon Valley companies. Her team prepared a sixty-five-question survey to gather benchmarking data and locate potential benchmark partners. Survey responses were summarized and provided to participating firms and to participants' management, and were published in a purchasing newsletter.

Twelve survey respondents attended a benchmarking round table held after the survey. In the MRO (maintenance repair operations) purchasing area, for example, roundtable participants shared their vision of the future in four topic areas: cost reduction,

MRO purchasing systems, innovative processes, and strategic directions. Useful continuous improvement ideas came up: One firm eliminated hard copy purchase orders for many expensed items up to $5,000, and planned to raise the base to $10,000. Credit cards were another way to eliminate invoicing and purchase orders. On-line requisition processing allows end users to place their own orders up to $5,000.

Rather than recommending to other benchmarkers specific books as guidelines, Ms. Williams recommends that team members invest in up-front planning and strategizing. "Be careful about picking what you measure. The volume of purchase requisitions processed by a buyer, for example, is an old rating, not appropriate for innovative supply management organizations." More important is the value of what a buyer does at her desk, not the volume of paper she can process in one day. Sun hires professionals who look at total value in purchasing: process improvements, quality, technology, and overall costs.

What are the relevant measures of excellent supply management at Sun? First, recommends Ms. Williams, look at how well a buyer has consolidated her supplier base. "If you have a family of twelve children, it's very hard to manage—you have a limited amount of time to spend with each one. But if you have four or fewer kids you can give each some individual attention. I look at [supplier management] the same way from the buyer's standpoint. If we can reduce the supplier base, we can really work with them to develop a more productive and efficient team. Many organizations expect buyers to manage a base of five hundred or more [suppliers]. Finding a realistic and workable number depends on the commodity. For a critical and complex commodity, because of the technology and the supplier development challenges, perhaps the ideal number is two, maybe only one. A buyer cannot manage an excess number of suppliers well."

Ms. Williams's advises benchmarkers from smaller companies to:

1. Establish a benchmarking team and carefully identify the desired outcome of the benchmarking project ("Don't just do it").
2. Locate companies in similar industries. It can, however, be helpful to go outside your industry if you understand the numbers and how to use the information.
3. Identify and move on actions to improve, and decide who will do it.

Kodak

Dave Goodwin, Kodak quality and industrial engineer, participated in a benchmarking project on technology innovation the objective was to determine the best way to identify technology for equipment manufacturing. Starting with the benchmarking model developed by Robert Camp at Xerox, the group modified their goal to look at innovation and cultures that nurture ideas. Their executive summary identified nine key factors that encourage innovation:

1. Cross-functional multi-involvement.
2. "Stewards" assigned to a specific technology, responsible for growth.
3. Customer-focused development processes.
4. Champions charged with implementing of new ideas.
5. Conscious efforts to put the right people in the right place. Sometimes people end up where they don't belong, and the group suffers as a result. Occasionally managers hesitate to release to new technology projects personnel who are "indispensable" to their departments.
6. Processes that support creativity, like idea generation sessions (which might seem to manufacturing pros like "the things marketing people do")
7. Natural outcomes that support innovation. Ask: "What happens to a new idea?," "What if?"

8. Expectation that engineers, for example, will keep up with new technology initiatives in their area.

9. Clear alignment with corporate initiatives and strategy.

Key insights from the benchmarking project, according to Goodwin, included how champions work. Every successful project has in one way or another been influenced by a champion. The "systems" within an organization (rewards, structure, measurement) must support and nurture innovation. The Kodak experience echoed Ken Stork's and Peggy Williams's advice to new benchmarkers: Up-front work is critical. Look at internal processes first, saving site visits and lengthy phone calls for last.

Honda of America (HAM)

After hosting over 400 companies in three years, Honda of America assembled a comprehensive benchmarking confab in April 1993, at its Marysville plant. Attended by over one hundred would-be benchmarkers, the two-day event was a hit. Tom Yashiki, HAM president, welcomed benchmarkers with "Please make any suggestions you have. We also want to learn from you."

Honda's very generous and open benchmarking policy produced a full menu of production topics for review, from procurement and production through quality, environmental practices, reward and recognition systems, and MIS to their innovative supplier development programs. Conference leader Dave Curry summarizes their attitude toward sharing this way: "All the things we do, we didn't invent them. It's *how* you do them, the commitment you bring to them—JIT, supplier development, the Deming circle—somebody else developed them, we just find a way to use them."

The company manages a full range of manufacturing, quality, and procurement functions. Within three years of auto production at Marysville, HAM became the fourth-largest auto manufacturer in the United States. The Marysville auto plant is fully integrated to include stamping, welding, painting, plastic injection molding, assembly, quality assurance, export, and other operations. Already recognized experts at engine buliding, Honda has increased local supplier parts content to 83 percent with its comprehensive supplier development programs. The company has, through its benchmarking and other supplier development practices, enabled many smaller companies to achieve world-class performance levels.

The Marysville auto assembly plant turns eighteen million dollars worth of inventory daily, with 1.5 to 1.7 days inventory in the pipeline, and one-half a day or less on the floor. East Liberty, where four- and two-door Civics are assembled, maintains two and a half hours of product on the floor. Honda's purchasing and tracking systems, soon to be supplemented with a new planning package from Japan called Target, are essential to maintain the company's aggressive JIT schedules. With ASN's (Advance Ship Notice), suppliers keep their customer informed of shipment status as shipments head to HAM headquarters. Three out of four suppliers are tied to the EDI (electronica data interchange) order and delivery systems. A major system goal for the next year is to eliminate "rip and read" paper purchase orders for all 246 suppliers, and to complete the automated payment system.

Conference attendees agreed there is no substitute for plant tours. When they follow initial research, benchmarking trips are invaluable because at world-class organizations like HAM, employees' behavior, the condition of the workplace, and other more subtle clues reveal much about company philosophy translated to day-to-day practice.

Benchmarking is a valuable partnering tool that allows a customer or supplier to measure its internal processes against those of the excellence models. The process of benchmarking also strengthens a group's external focus, another aid to the partnering exercise. But benchmarking as a process is only a quality tool, one of several valuable partnering tools. When misused as an uncontrolled or unplanned exploration exercise, it loses its punch. Benchmarking exercises fail when they

- become "fun" trips with minimal preparation
- do not include a commitment to follow-up improvement efforts from the benchmarkers themselves, as well as their supporting management team
- benchmark the wrong topic

Organizations that select a few strategic areas to benchmark at the beginning of the process have more successes and will be welcomed back the next time they want to compare notes.

Remember that not all growth and innovation in U. S. industry will come from the former blue chip giants. Smaller businesses and start-ups will be responsible for most new job creation. For these groups, manufacturing networks are essential for growth and benchmarking is an essential, cost-effective tool for their continuous improvement.

NOTES

1. Greg Watson, *The Benchmarking Workbook* (Portland, Ore: Productivity Press, 1992), p. 12.

2. Ken Stork, book review, *Target*, July–August 1992, p. 44.

CHAPTER 5

Looking to the Next Tier: Contract Manufacturing and Outsourcing

Steve Jobs's second start-up, NeXT Computer, has shuttered its highly automated Fremont, California, factory ("the machine that makes the machine.)" Designed and built at a cost of millions, to produce perfect printed circuit boards every time, the NeXT factory was a laboratory for many new manufacturing techniques that will, as they are adopted by other producers, help make product faster and better than ever before. NeXT proved that final assembly and test plants could produce zero defects. Product design was engineered for manufacturability; their cpu (central processing unit) "pizza" box design was easily assembled and quickly disassembled. The Fremont plant solved several environmental design problems—human and chemical—long before the competition figured them out. Robots, vision systems, Phd. factory workers, all the elements of the NeXT factory system design pointed toward the future. So what went wrong?

A lot of things never went right. The sad story of the demise of the NeXT experiment is that the market moved too quickly. First-product introductions were expensive, limited, and adopted mostly by expert users. Although later offerings well loved by the same experts, particularly those in the academic/laboratory community, they never took a strong hold in the commercial world where issues of market channels, operating systems, competitor pricing, and simplicity won over features that Jobs hoped would sell themselves.

CORE COMPETENCIES

Randy Heffner, Hewlett-Packard veteran and former vice president of operations at NeXT, wanted the experiment to succeed. He hoped to prove that a beautifully designed, innovative approach to manufacturing—all functions in one location—would work. His "personal competition," Sun Microsystems, a few miles down the road in Palo Alto, was battling for the same marketplace, the desk-top work station, with a very different strategy. Sun's gameplan, production of final assemblies supplied by a network of subcontractors, would allow them to develop their own core competencies.

Core competencies are those skills that exemplify an organization's true expertise. As many cash-rich companies discovered in the eighties, when there was a spate of diversification into unfamiliar technologies and market channels, sticking to known business makes sense and often yields more profit. The principle of core competencies requires careful identification of the areas where a business naturally excels—the core areas—and the functions that should be outsourced. Many industries begin with vertical integration—the company does everything, from raw material to after-market service—and "unvertically integrate" when profitability problems arise or barriers to entry drop.

For example, both U.S. Steel and Digital Equipment Company (DEC), were vertically integrated in their heyday, controlling supplies of upstream raw materials—ore and railroads in the case of U.S. Steel (now USX), and cables and chips for DEC. DEC's idea was to guarantee component supply for its main market penetration products. Digital's Springfield, Massachusetts, facility may not have been the cheapest or the most reliable cable assembly supplier, but it was *theirs*.

What is Vertical Integration?: Vertical integration is the inclusion in one company's operations of all the activities that bring a product to market. In the manufacturing and marketing of gasoline, a vertically integrated company would explore and purchase mineral rights to the land under which the oil lies; drill the well and pump oil from it; transport the crude oil from well to refinery; refine the crude oil into petroleum products; transport refined gas from refinery to storage tanks, then to service stations; and sell gasoline at the service station pump.[1]

Sun Microsystems took the opposite view, placing the emphasis on outsourcing. Outsourcing advantages include flexibility, lower cost, and—with good partners—increased technical input from suppliers ("the experts" in their field) during critical design stages. Sun planned to continue to focus on their core competency by offering a platform miles ahead of competitors' products in speed and features. The company grew fast by introducing a barrage of new, faster products to the engineering market, DEC's old stomping ground. Sun chose to depend on suppliers to produce high-quality components, which Sun then packaged with software. The strategy was to capture the engineering market lost by DEC's VAX's. After all, would the workstation user really care whether Sun or an outside supplier made that monitor, or even her motherboard? Sun built a network of high-quality suppliers dedicated to helping their customer capture more market.

NeXT, on the other hand, continued to perfect their showcase factory to manufacture systems, but never captured the volume to fill their high-tech assembly line. And DEC encountered problems with late new-product introductions as their competitors advanced.

The Sun network approach worked, as it continues to work for other organizations like EMC and Seagate, Solectron and Exabyte, Honda, Apple, Xyplex, PictureTel, and numerous less well-known smaller enterprises. Each of these winners has chosen to dedicate its finite human, financial, and creative resources to offering the best *end* product *before* a German, or Japanese, or Korean competitor does. Speed and flexibility count. These companies chose not to spend their money on elegant automation and innovative equipment. Instead, they invested in human capital that *obtained* the best components and then moved rapidly into final assembly and value-added services. They contract parts of the production cycle to the "second tier" of suppliers, those companies one or more steps removed in the supply chain from the integration of product, the step closest to end customers.

"LET'S GET SMALL." (Steve Martin)

Networked manufacturing is an alternative to big, inflexible, vertically integrated companies, as many onetime blue chip giants have recently discovered. Their stocks, the cushions that your parents hoped would take them through retirement, have lost value. The big, high-volume organizations that absorbed generations of immigrants and their children have changed names or become otherwise unrecognizable. Even the Dow Jones Industrial Average, that calculation of the health of a few dozen blue chips, a number that registered how well we were doing for so many years, is being redesigned.

The U.S. industrial landscape, like its organizations themselves, used to be organized in supply chain hierarchies, or *tiers*. Each small foundry was a supplier to another group of small or medium-sized companies that were suppliers to the giants; the hierarchy grew in resources and power as one moved up the chain. Bunched at the bottom of the hierarchy were the suppliers who, unless they held sole source commodity control, scrambled to accommodate customer requirements.

The big companies managed contract manufacturing and purchasing administration with a heavy hand. Usually a single purchasing buyer was awarded the task of juggling several subcontract houses; if that buyer handled no other suppliers, he became an outsider within his own planning group, probably spending twice as much time on the road as his colleagues.

Fifteen years ago contract manufacturers sat at the bottom of the pyramid and were strongly influenced by events at the apex. For example, many suppliers to the computer industry suffered when the plants they supplied folded. Calcomp, a New Hampshire printed circuit board house, was one of them. At one time Calcomp dedicated over 30 percent of its high-volume manufacturing capacity to IBM; when IBM and Digital stumbled, Calcomp fell.

Now owned by Lockheed, the company is conducting a war on three fronts. To regain a strong position the company must simultaneously recast its manufacturing facility, its customer base, and its work force. It has dismissed one-third of its work force and is redesigning its manufacturing operations to be more flexible and offer quick turnaround on small production runs. As the company restructured its work force and created small product cells, it also recrafted its strategy. Its principal objective is to offer high quality and speed to an assortment of customers located within a ninety-mile radius (one to two hours away).

In contract manufacturing quality is a given, according to Jim Bell, Lockheed's vice president of business development. If a company is not producing acceptable products consistently, customers will go elsewhere. "You're only as good as your last shipment—

memories are not very long," he notes. Changing a second-tier board shop to a world-class turnkey supplier is, as Lockheed discovered, an uphill struggle.

Many small contract manufacturers won't make it through the massive industry restructuring and downturns. They must fight offshore and domestic competition for a toehold with healthy customers. Many contract manufacturers have inherited outdated equipment; most have neglected work-force development. Some suppliers to the computer giants and GM, unable to acquire new, healthy customers or quickly develop new products, are already in a downward spiral. To survive, such companies must create new supplier relationships.

When manufacturers like Sun became service providers and idea generators as well as product assemblers and software developers, their subcontract suppliers assumed more importance, and, what was previously a hierarchy became a network of temporarily linked customers and suppliers. Even big computer companies were affected. As they took themselves out of the vertical integration configuration, they came to rely more on smaller suppliers for quality products and even design suggestions.

Dependence on contract manufacturing can pose new risks that were unknown with internal "captive" producers. Internal production (vertical integration) usually costs more, but it is more reliable than using a subcontractor with whom a customer has not worked out a good partnership arrangement. Contract manufacturing requires especially clean, fast communication networks. Customers and suppliers, however, must recognize that the only substitute for blue chip reliability is strong linkages and direct communications.

IBM is one of the giants moving as quickly as it can from vertical integration to linked enterprises. Market swings caused this radical paradigm shift. Until the late 1980s, IBM "made the market." Its organizational structure and communication lines were designed to support forward penetration of its newest products. Unfortunately, the company's rigidity and layers of management made for an entity that could not be light on its feet in the face of customer changes. Big Blue's response has been to rearrange its own body parts, hoping to create a new enterprise network of profitable small businesses. Digital has attempted the same type of restructuring, but as would be expected from its matrix-management organization, the process is slower and muddled.

FIGURE 5.1: Vertical Integration—Advantages and Disadvantages

Vertical Integration Model

1. **U.S. STEEL:** From ore to railroads and barge carriers for ore, to processing mills, to warehouses
2. **INTERNATIONAL PAPER:** Androscoggin, fully integrated, from pulp and some timber holdings, through paper manufacturing
3. **DIGITAL EQUIPMENT CORPORATION:** Feeder plants supply assembly plants with cables, connectors, boards, power supplies, monitors, disk drives, tape drives, etc.

ADVANTAGES	DISADVANTAGES
• Control of supply, no anticipated breaks in pipeline. • Proprietary technology "stays home."	• Organization becomes jack-of-all-trades. • Requires much capital. • High entry barriers as hierarchy grows. • The organization becomes less flexible. • Heavy investment in capital equipment drives organization to stay with older products and technologies.

GIANT'S POWER MAGNIFIED AT SECOND-TIER LEVEL

General Electric, with its "We will be number one" criterion, regularly cleans its closets by selling off less profitable divisions. But General Electric does not do everything right. The company has chosen not to base its supply management strategy on building a strong network of customer-supplier partners dedicated to quality, continuous improvement, and lastly, price. Following the GM example, some GE managers have taken the Lopez approach to suppliers, demanding 20 and 30 percent price cuts per line item. This policy lowers costs, but it does not encourage a cooperative long-term approach to mutual market success, as does the Honda target pricing exercise. Micromanaging suppliers à la GM and GE forces supply management professionals to concentrate on the details of purchase price variances, rather than on the development of supplier capabilities and improved communications.

There is further fallout from the GM-Lopez approach. When big suppliers "get tough" with smaller upstream suppliers, the effect of their heavy-handed treatment is magnified in the smaller companies. A $2-million-dollar plastics supplier will certainly be hurt more by unreasonable customer demands than would an internal GE plastics division ten or twenty times larger. The $2-million-dollar company has less buffer and fewer resources to deal with customer demands; personnel are stretched more to cover scheduling, production, and quality/design issues. When a purchasing manager is forced by his customer to spend three to six hours a day reviewing line item costs on purchase orders, his focus naturally strays from quality and continuous improvement teaming.

Second-tier suppliers basically have only two response options to such tactics: find a new customer, or cut corners. According to another GM parts supplier, six months after the Lopez hard-line cost edicts came down, they had no other choice but to "put unqualified parts in the bin. If that's the way they want to treat us, this is what they will get." Would you buy a car from this type of "partner"?

CONTRACT MANUFACTURERS SAY, "TAKE THE HIGH ROAD."

Xerox and Motorola have long had good reputations for supplier development and partnering, each for different reasons. Seitz Corporation, a Connecticut plastics supplier for Xerox, credits Xerox with saving the business. President Alan Seitz remembers the days before the turnaround:

> We were typical of most manufacturers. Many large U.S. OEM's [original equipment manufacturer] were very naive. I remember one in particular. In their [the company's] . . . 1984 financial statement, the board of directors was photographed in full yellow rain gear with the caption "We weathered the storm." . . . When there was a problem, we went from problem to solution without fully analyzing the root cause, and the fix was a Band-aid. We learned a lot from Xerox, one of our major customers. Many other large OEM's were offering processes like their quality training to their suppliers. We reviewed them all, but none offered as much depth as Xerox's, and it came for free.

Convinced the company needed to look for new product and market opportunities, Seitz was among a group of Xerox suppliers invited to a Total Quality gathering in 1987. A team of twelve Seitz personnel made the trip, coming back with fresh insights on benchmarking and Total Quality approaches. Employees joined up, some sceptical at first; all were formally trained in problem solving and other quality and team skills. First team efforts included intensive benchmarking, learned from the Xerox experts who pioneered the process. Seitz attributes a 20 percent increase in productivity in 1991 to the Total Quality commitment. Other favorable results include big sales increases (from $19 million in 1991 to $25 million in 1992) and the introduction of several new products.

CONTRACT MANUFACTURERS' SPECIAL REQUIREMENTS

In addition to the good practices of innovative supply managers, small companies clearly have special networking and pooled resource needs. Contract manufacturers must have three strengths: leadership, communications, and people.

Strength No. 1: Dynamic, Creative Leadership

For smaller partners, management leadership makes all the difference. Nypro, EMC, Sun, and Solectron are generally considered to be blessed with visionary leadership. Mike Schoonover of EMC, Gordon Lankton, president of Nypro, Winston Chen and Ko Nishimura of Solectron, and Scott McNealy of Sun are dynamic managers who have made their companies first-class competitors. Their charismatic management styles are legendary within their organizations, and outside, the myths grow.

Each of these leaders has a strong entrepreneurial streak. Lankton is unafraid of hiring entrepreneurial managers, then setting them up in small businesses when they get restless. "You have to be an entrepreneur in this business. It's a job shop business where decisions must be made instantaneously all day long. Customers call and ask for things, sometimes the challenge is materials, sometimes process. We know that if we can't do it, someone else will."

Winston and Ko of Solectron dreamed big from the start. They hired, trained, and rewarded performance that grew Solectron beyond it's board supplier beginnings. Quality goals were set at world-class levels to stretch organizational capabilities. Like other second-tier leaders, as the companies grew, they tended to set up small regionalized facilities, rather than adding to one central plant. This "McDonald's approach to manufacturing" encourages the entrepreneurial spirit.

Each of these leaders is a superb communicator, and each has an abiding interest and pride in developing people. Lankton's approach to linking board structure with the need for management development is unique:

> We think Nypro's working boards of directors for each plant contribute to continuous improvement. Each six-member board is put together with individuals with the particular talent needed for that site, sometimes production people, sometimes engineers, sometimes sales people, etc. People love to serve on the boards, although there is no monetary reward. We tell the board members, "The general manager reports to you, and your job is to help him make this plant successful." We don't expect one general manager to have all the capabilities it takes to run the plant, but the board allows access to them, and board members feel responsibility for that plant. If the plant gets in trouble, they become advocates throughout Nypro to get help.

Solectron, a West Coast board supplier and Baldrige Award winner, has from the start focused on becoming a world-class manufacturer like the world-class customers it supplies: Apple, Hewlett-Packard, and Sun. Failing to win the Baldrige on its first attempt, the company learned from its weaknesses, two of which were community involvement and communications. Managers developed a program to strengthen these areas, both of which required people and money. To Solectron's people, communications represents far more than a check on the Baldrige application, however. Communications skill is the *only* way for the company to manage complex, fast-moving long-distance partnerships.

Solectron attacks specific problems with communications. Like

Nypro, Solectron does not seek to insulate itself from negative feedback. Their Tuesday-Wednesday-Thursday meeting series features one morning of customer feedback based on their Customer Satisfaction Index (CSI), a document that elicits specific customer-supplier exchanges. (See Resource 1.) Another day's production meeting is dedicated just to quality.

The intent at Solectron is to take supplier management beyond simple procurement. Jeff Bloch, Solectron director of supply base management, describes this maturation beyond traditional contract manufacturing deals. "It's the next step going from a transaction-based relationship to a tactical-based, broad, complete process orientation, including everything from the selection process, measurement, the categories in which we rate suppliers, and the whole relationship issue." Bloch's group tries to build a mix of technical and materials or procurement skills. For a function that does not have a large staff, the most important skill for supply management success is team leadership.

Bloch's three and a half years with Intel in Japan taught him a few lessons in partnering. The Japanese approach to supply management is fundamentally relationship-based; very little is written into a contract. Partnerships are based on historical relationships in an environment in which customers are very demanding. The Japanese approach can work in the U.S. only if the customer understands what makes the *supplier* successful, not just what makes the customer successful. Bloch summarizes the meaning of this shift for second-tier suppliers: "Customers have to understand, there will be a limited number of world-class suppliers, and customers will be competing for their capabilities—it's already happening in some electronic commodity groups." The customer that can attract and hold a world-class supplier's attention has a strategic advantage. Customers must think beyond surface partnership issues—forecasting and scheduling, for example—to really understand what makes suppliers successful. Two points are key to that understanding:

- The customer must be clear on expectations.
- The customer must listen to the supplier.

Bloch's Intel experience reinforced the importance of listening well. Intel took the initiative to listen to its partner advice and formed the Supplier Partnership Program, a structured approach to partnering that has lasted ten years. Translated to the Solectron environment, listening to suppliers in the beginning stages of partnership development included sending a survey to major suppliers. Administered through a third party, the questionnaire serves to "baseline reality," to establish needs and gaps between what partners say vs. what they do. The objective is to reach beyond the surface partnership talk that is often used as a selling point. Customers want to know that their communications will be effectively used.

Strength No. 2: Communications

Initially, someone must act as a facilitator, a third party who tracks both sides of the partnership and facilitates communications, as in the Solectron example above. The Japanese don't tend to provide much direct feedback, and so Bloch's role during his tenure in the Japanese plant was to help maintain the relationship, an approach he stresses at Solectron.

Communications linkages work well for smaller organizations only if they demonstrate an integrated, consistent philosophy toward customers and suppliers. Watch out for disconnects within organizations. Bloch notes how companies approach partnerships—what they do on the customer (marketing) and supplier (materials management/production) sides are frequently totally different. (Or there may be a yawning gap between the material side and the marketing side of the business).

Solectron's supplier survey minimizes the "internal disconnects." After the data are compiled, feedback sessions and action steps are scheduled in what Solectron calls its Supplier

Symposium. This forum focuses internal attention on consistency and reinforces its commitment to suppliers: "Here's what you said, here're the data, and let us tell you what we are doing to address your concerns."

Critical to Solectron's success as a supplier is its effectiveness in aligning its operations with its customers'. In their contract manufacturing business, Solectron buys components from the customer's approved manufacturer list. Buying the majority of components from customer-specified suppliers adds a whole new level of complexity to partnering by contractors, a level not generally encountered in first-tier organizations.

Strength No. 3: People

Xyplex is a Massachusetts network equipment assembler with a small supply management organization. The company's heavy dependence on its subcontractors makes the job of subcontract administration critical. Reporting to the Director of Materials, the professional filling this slot is first of all a superb communicator; the other "technical" skills are simply assumed to be there—a big change from the traditional purchasing buyer role. Here are the requirements for subcontract administration supervisor as described by the company's subcontract manager:

> A bachelor's business degree, eight years purchasing or inventory control experience, experience with computer planning systems, professional certification (APICS or NAPM), and excellent written, verbal, negotiation and interpersonal skills.

QUALITY FOR SUBCONTRACT MANUFACTURING

Manufacturing firms, especially those in high tech, will continue to outsource many of their components, rendering their own facilities' assembly and software units extinct. They cannot operate without excellent subcontract partnerships as their subcontractors increasingly become an extension of the customer's own manufacturing cycle. Qualification and certification of supplier material thus are also increasingly important—and here special attention must be paid to the process of quality assurance. Organizational unifiers like standard audits are only the beginning, serving to help achieve acceptable levels of quality.

As a basic requirement, quality performance expectations must be expressed quantitatively because most suppliers must service more than one customer. For sheer simplicity, customers should make it easy for suppliers to excel by using rigorous (but not unrealistic) quality specifications.

Netcomm, a network equipment assembler, published the supplier expectation list in Figure 5.2 as a model of clear communications. The agreement covers eight areas of customer concern, not all of which are expressed quantitatively. Some areas leave room for movement, but their inclusion in the agreement guarantees periodic discussion.

IN SEARCH OF A SINGLE STANDARD

Today, companies are still struggling with numerous quality audits, but not too many years down the road, innovative enterprises should be able to consult a standardized performance audit, the way we now access financial performance in Dun & Bradstreet to select both suppliers and customers. Small companies especially need useful, standardized data on product/process quality, a key indicator for contract manufacturers.

Currently, a number of quality certification audits are available, some of which are more enthusiastically offered than others. Examples include the Baldrige Award, Shingo, ISO 9000, and Motorola's QSR. For a small company, or even a big one with resource limitations, duplication of audits is more than a misuse of human capital. Multiple audits are a distraction that pull key employees

FIGURE 5.2: A Model Customer-Supplier Agreement

NETCOMM SUPPLIER REQUIREMENTS

1. Quality—Suppliers are to demonstrate continuous process and quality improvements with the support and assistance of Netcomm. A 96% or greater yield on boards is expected.

2. Delivery—On-time delivery is expected. Once a learning curve has been established, a nine-day turnaround on boards is required (nine days from receipt of a complete kit).

3. Partnering—Netcomm works closely with suppliers to develop process improvements and direct cost reduction efforts, as appropriate. Netcomm expects suppliers to work with us in attaining these objectives.

4. Process improvement—Netcomm encourages all suppliers to provide input with respect to process improvements or changes that can be made at Netcomm. For example, if Netcomm can improve the quality of kits or provide better documentation to our suppliers, we look for the opportunity to do so. Creating an awareness of such improvements will provide better results.

5. Customer service—Netcomm expects a high level of customer service. Suppliers must be responsive to addressing questions or concerns as they arise. One contact person at the supplier is preferred.

6. Buffer stock—Netcomm provides a 3 percent buffer stock on capacitors and resistors. This material is expected to cover any damage incurred in the auto-insertion process.

7. Source inspection—All boards are source inspected by Netcomm prior to shipment. Suppliers are asked to adhere to the directions specified of our quality representative at the on-site source inspection.

8. Qualification process—Small lot sizes, buffer stock, documentation review meeting, turnaround on qualification boards, and lead times for qualification kits.

into projects that generally offer little added value. Small manufacturers (fewer than five hundred employees) account for 98 percent of the United States' 358,000 manufacturing firms, employing eight million workers, or 40 percent of the workforce.[2] Over the next decade, small and medium-sized producers will account for 90 percent of new job growth. These organizations don't have the duplicate staffs to deal with duplicate quality routines!

ISO 9000 is not the answer. (The audit is based on standards laid down by the International Organization for Stardardization, the name is based on the Greek *isos*, or "equal.") Described in Europe as simply a driver's license, ISO registration tells the customer little about a supplier's ability to produce a quality product; it simply "puts him on the road." The emphasis on documentation—ring binders filled with paper—is a guarantee that many trees will die in the name of ISO registration.

Other quality assessments hold similar pitfalls. The Baldrige Award application process *can* be used as a continuous improvement tool, but the application takes time and money. And until recently, Baldrige Awards failed to assess financial viability. Several winners have hit the skids. Although the Motorola Quality System Review is a comprehensive, easy-to-administer document, its scores are not accepted as an industry standard. The fact is, smaller companies seldom have time for more than a single continuous improvement initiative. When suppliers start working on ISO registration, they put other worthwhile improvement efforts on hold.

Some solutions to the plethora of quality audits have been suggested, but for now, suppliers can only hope to persuade customers to simplify their lives by accepting a single quality audit, as supplier Molex has with customers NCR, Motorola, and Xerox. (See also Chapter 10 "On Being a World-Class Customer.")

In *The Soul of the Enterprise*, Robert W. Hall comments on the pattern of growth the United States has experienced since the first inhabitants pushed from coastal and river-landing settlements into open lands and forests. Then the frontier was limitless—you just had to be there to grow. Unfortunately, growth for the sake of growth is an unreliable and unrealistic strategy, especially for smaller companies. To survive and prosper in today's world, Hall advises companies to look beyond growth for growth's sake— "just making things"—to growth for the sake of profitability. The winners will seek out phases of the manufacturing process rich with strong margins. For second-tier suppliers in the printed circuit board sector, this niche is not board fabrication, assembly, and test; it is value-added customer services: "turnkey" offerings, from design, prototyping, and supplier sourcing through full production and even software development. The winners establish niches to lock on to particular customers, and their product offerings will reinforce the bond. In this scenario, it should be hard to buy a new supplier.

The old vision of growth that continually fed and absorbed thousands of new settlers has disappeared from the American business landscape. America cannot compete with third-world countries in volume and technology as it did through the 1960's. Manufacturing excellence is transportable; it works equally well in Singapore or Cleveland. Opportunity occurs, as it did for the immigrants, in various forms. In seventeenth-century Newbury, Massachusetts, the English law of primogeniture meant that generally all property went to the first-born son. Other siblings thus had great incentive to move from areas where all the land had been surveyed and parceled out to what was then the far west, one or two days' wagon ride out. A century later, land grants to Revolutionary War veterans fostered the development of the New Hampshire, Vermont, and western Massachusetts "frontier." Later bursts driven by economic need settled the Midwest, followed by the Pacific coast lands. Each time land got scarce, a new burst of outward expansion and growth followed.

This pattern describes the new forms of profitable market expansion that networked manufacturing partners must uncover or create for themselves. They cannot depend on big institutions—unions, governments, professional groups, or customers—to do it for them.

Like some other large institutions that seemed to be permanent fixtures, first-tier giants will be in disarray for another decade. Companies must look to the second-tier for growth and profitability. To successfully rebuild the industrial base with smaller organizations it's important to address these two issues:

1. U.S. companies must look to each other for strength by partnering for collective enterprise advantage with both small and large companies.
2. Small and medium-sized businesses must find ways to build internal excellence into their manufacturing, supply management, design, work-force development, and customer management processes. Where their resources are limited, they need to partner with others, or learn from their customers.

The term "second tier" means that the company is one step removed from the end customer. But "second tier" does not imply "second rate." Second-tier companies must leapfrog that distance by practicing excellence with the same dedication that bigger organizations like Honda and Motorola do. Unfortunately, the second tier doesn't get second chances; all improvement efforts, therefore, must be right the first time. Small size is a clear advantage, however, when it prevents a company from picking up unwieldy, rigid organizational structures and over-specialized functions.

NOTES

1. Roger W. Schmenner, *Production/Operations Management, from the Inside Out* (New York: Macmillan, 1993), p. 487.

2. National Center for Manufacturing Sciences, *Focus*, November 1992, p. 1–2.

FURTHER READING

For further reading on the special requirements of small or subcontract manufacturers, see:

Robert W. Hall, *The Soul of the Enterprise* (New York: HarperCollins, 1993).

Liz Mitchell, "The EMC Story," in *On Achieving Excellence* (newsletter published by the Tom Peters Group, Berkeley, California), fall 1993.

Lea Tonkin, "The Power of Total Quality at Seitz Corporation," *Target*, Winter 1991, pp. 6–12.

CHAPTER 6

Partnering Planning and Control Systems—Simple Systems for Smart People

*W*hat was this mysterious "alligator" I'd been hearing about? Where was the secretive creature hiding himself? My partner and I had been doing some systems work, a facelift for an old IBM planning and scheduling system, taking a nip here and a tuck there— some invisible stitches that would tie the whole mess together. The flowchart showed a tangled "before" and a somewhat clearer "after" picture of data moving from customer request through purchasing and production control down into the shop. But the numbers never added up. The final shipment figure was always less than the first input to the system. We followed the trail of crumbs back to a stopping point in the middle of the process, to the desk of an always busy Irishman. Systems are designed to work perfectly, but they usually don't. That's where Mr. O'Brien appeared to magically resolve conflicts between customer demand (too much, too soon), and production. Mr. O'Brien made the tough decisions that the system could not. In the flow chart his cubicle was labeled "the Allocator." My ears and the grapevine had distorted his nickname to "the alligator."

Where the system hit disconnects, where the trade-offs between customer demands and production capabilities needed human judgment, the ground softened and data disappeared into the mud. That's where The Allocator came in. This system could not have operated without The Allocator.

THE FUTURE OF PARTNERING = THE FUTURE OF SYSTEMS

Linked customers and suppliers, networked manufacturing, bits of scheduling and customer-designed data flying over 24,000 baud modems from showroom to shipping bay are not that far in the future. The computer industry's stolid defense, followed by its pressured abandonment of proprietary software parallels the changes customers and suppliers demand now from computer networks. That industry belatedly addressed the limitations of proprietary software designed to lock customers into specific hardware suppliers. Within a few years proprietary software turned from a benefit—an easy way for customers to grow their systems—to a stone around the neck. When customers shopped for software, they dropped their inflexible, application-limited proprietary package. Data General, Digital Equipment Corporation, Apollo, and others ran through the initial advantages of proprietary products within ten years of their founding. When users moved to smaller and faster system components, their previously all Big Blue or all DEC houses required networking gurus, high-tech translators, to make the pieces talk to each other. And when even the gurus couldn't force an IBM plug into an Apple socket, end-user customers were forced to maintain redundant and frequently unfriendly competitor systems.

INTEGRATION

The same integration issues appear as customers and suppliers begin system linkages for selected information sharing. Fortunately, partial networking solutions are already available, and complete systems with seamless plug and play capabilities will be here by 1995 or earlier. For now, the integration problem extends beyond the obvious failure of MRP commercial and in-house packages to talk to each other, because the systems of truly integrated enterprises will go far beyond material requirements planning and logistics trackers. The best network integration utilities will offer additional features to eliminate paperwork and facilitate design, while speeding the transfer of essential customer information. They will speak in a language common to designers, supply managers, and manufacturing professionals. The data base structure that supports users' needs will offer flexibility and varying amounts of detail for many functional needs throughout the integrated enterprise.

Manufacturing over the next five to ten years will become leaner and more flexible, as will the systems that tie the pieces together. Production of major assemblies will be in *days*; components of short-cycle times will be in *hours*. Three-day cars, four-day houses, three-day silicon wafers highlight the speed and agility required of integrated, open systems, without which products suffer through lengthy hand-offs and conversions. Texas Instruments is prototyping a complete silicon wafer production system that experts say changes the way the semiconductor industry makes chips. Instead of producing big batches of wafers in a multi-million-dollar clean-room facility, Cecil Davis and other engineers at TI have created an Advanced Vacuum Processor device supported by a CIM (computer-integrated manufacturing) system to produce single-wafer batches in *days*. (They put the "clean room" in the equipment.) The CIM system will close the loop between customer order, scheduling, and shipment.

We are not far from complete integration of customer orders into supplier systems. Some companies, Bose among them, ask suppliers to enter orders directly. But the last few pieces of the puzzle are the most difficult. To meet customer and supplier user needs, software and network technology products must include five basic systems features:

1. **A flexible and fast "front-end"** that can be accessed by procurement as well as design and manufacturing engineering. Ideally, the software for the "front end" would take, for example, a car from concept through design to prototype and full production via a single software package.
2. **Planning modules,** including MRP, to explode orders or forecasts into component and raw material requirements, as part of long-range planning.
3. **Procurement software** to track supplier performance (quality and shipments).
4. **Scheduling module** enabling master schedules or supplier schedules to be transmitted directly to the customer production line are best maintained on a computer linked with other planning information.
5. **Network utilities** that tie together some but not all customer and supplier scheduling and technical or engineering information. This category includes EDI software.

1. The "Front End"

Everything that happens before materials planning, well before production starts, resides in various manual and automated systems in the "front end." Today, these systems typically include CAD/CAM (computer-aided design/computer-aided manufacturing) and various linkages to material planning. They may also link designs to tooling, but no packages are commercially available that integrate all these functions.

As production and procurement get leaner and more flexible, however, and as these operations cut time out of the cycle, the big time and cost reduction opportunities appear earlier upstream, where designers commit significant material, capital equipment, and process costs to a particular design or technology. The farther upstream system integration reaches—approaching the designer's desk—the more difficult it is to integrate procurement with design operations. Design and procurement speak different languages, usually use different tools and systems, and seldom team up. The auto industry's complex and lengthy concept-to-production cycle is getting shorter; systems are now the only limitation to system integration.

Car stylists don't like CAD/CAM systems. They are too mechanical, like asking an artist to paint with mechanical drawing tools. CAD/CAM systems are typically not the source of procurement information. And by the time a design has moved to a CAD/CAM system, it may be too late to benefit from procurement input. The auto and computer/semiconductor sectors are, therefore, prime candidates to tie procurement, design, and manufacturing people together.

According to Douglas Glasson, a design systems integration expert at TASC in Reading, Massachusetts, the "old way" of designing vehicles is a maze of hand-offs and loop-backs. First, product planners create goals for a vehicle on the basis of societal studies or demographics. The planners hand off product goals to the design group. At this point most issues concern styling, so engineering team members are minimally involved, perhaps providing rough volumetric requirements (hood clearance for the engine, passenger space, amount of glass). Designers' sketches then pass through design competitions and reviews that narrow down the choices to two or three. The next step might be fiberglass mock-ups for auto shows to elicit consumer feedback. At this point the car's styling and envelope and some performance (engine, suspension, and transmission) characteristics are set.

From a clay model the designers transfer coordinates to paper. A few more steps—fixing little design problems and other changes—and the complex process progresses finally to surface tooling. No wonder even the shortest production cycle seems long!

Glasson cites Chrysler and Volvo as being well on the way to solving the challenge of integrating and shortening the whole process. Both have made considerable innovations in the design process. Volvo's Los Angeles design studio has completed two designs, one an environmental concept car and one a production car, substituting a software package called *Alias* for the traditional clay model steps.

Chrysler uses traditional sketches for conceptualizing designs. Engineers then build computer models from the sketches to create a full-size clay model. Designers find it easier to sketch with pencil and paper than a mouse and a screen. At the Art Center for Creative Studies in Pasadena, California, an approach similar to Volvo's design studio's is being taught. Students do conceptual designs on the computer and then rely on some version of automatic model building to realize the final design.

Volvo's revolutionary approach is faster and involves fewer design personnel. It satisfies the problem caused by the fact that companies cannot *force* various functions to use another department's software package; this software meets interdepartmental team requirements.

The *Alias* package pricetag, approximately $90,000, is partly justified by the fact that system data are recyclable. The system will also generate files to drive numerically controlled metal cutting machines, and to create mechanical drawings, thereby taking more time out of the design-to-production cycle. The beauty of the software is that it takes time-consuming steps out of the process, and it has achieved success among stylists and engineers alike. This type of software is a perfect vehicle for early supply management involvement because it contains some, but not yet all, design data that procurement needs for earlier supplier sign-ups.

Internal planning and control systems

Most commercial packages still need "fixing" to facilitate partnership linkages between customers and suppliers. They are typically data- or transaction-intensive when they should be more visual, and the systems do not integrate well because of proprietary software problems. Security is also problematic; partners need the ability to selectively open sections of their system to partners. And the biggest failing is that systems are not integrated *internally* so that procurement people can make decisions based on consistent information from all departments, derived from the same data base.

Hewlett-Packard, long a leader in progressive planning and control systems, is developing solutions to that problem. In the early eighties, the company changed its planning system from one that featured traditional buying tasks to one that accommodated commodity teams. HP's procurement system, PROMIS (*pro*curement *mis*) standardized interdivisional activities like purchase orders. The system also automated many clerical tasks. But PROMIS itself is now being supplemented with third-party modules to meet HP's current and future challenges, including cost reduction and time-to-market.

According to Marsha Begun, HP's director of procurement processes, the company now needs a planning system that will decrease its time-to-market combined with lowest costs. "What we really need is a new kind of information system that spans the *entire* product generation process—everything from the idea to the business planning stage at the highest level of management to marketing, R&D, and manufacturing, distribution, and finally support and obsolescence." The planning process begins at the initial design and prototype stage, through first production and final production.

This new system must offer each function all the information it needs to maximize design. Purchasers, for example, need component information that differs from typical designers' needs such as physical characteristics, parametrics, and tolerances. Marketing does not need the same technical information, but in order to work with designers, marketing needs to know microprocessor speed and performance capability, memory size, and component pricing.

The planning system should allow both marketing and R&D to work in parallel from a common information base. When these functions work "in separate rooms," the results are often unfortunate. The story of HP's failed calculator watch illustrates the danger of segregating design from marketing and production.

Several years ago the HP calculator division had the bright idea of producing a wristwatch that incorporated a calculator. Evidently, marketing and design failed to collaborate on the idea, even though the concept and technical capabilities were available in-house. The finished product was large and heavy and needed "downsizing" to fit the average human wrist. Since then, the company has learned how to reduce size, as evidenced by its hand-held personal computer, and design, marketing, procurement, and production working together have racked up a series of new product successes.

The bigger challenge for all enterprises is system integration to facilitate standardization and design. Begun sums it up this way: "Enterprises will not lose their functional silos until their systems do." The term "design for procurement" expresses the ideal situation in which, say, a printed circuit board designer would design-in devices preferred by procurement. The designer would also know which processes were available in production, as she designed the board. Design for procurement further implies that designers select recommended suppliers who will offer superb quality, timely delivery, the on-target price, and environmentally correct product designs.

Production machine requirements, part numbering schemes,

local configurations (European vs. American), add-on require-ments for cables, power supplies, and keyboards—all are issues that require inclusion in the system. Field service and other after-market groups are currently seldom included in the data base, but a company cannot best serve customers unless it is integrated into the system. HP procurement chief Gene Richter's goal, "to have a buyer sitting at the designer's elbow," requires total system integration.

2. *Planning Modules*

Before companies link their systems to those of customers and suppliers, internal planning and control methods must be as simple and seamless as is technically feasible. Advanced planning systems all need the ability to break down finished requirements into components and raw material demand, the bill of material explosion feature that resides in the heart of an MRP package.

Here is where MRP systems, when they are overused, get in the way. Internally, excellent suppliers and excellent customers need powerful, but flexible systems. Companies like Solectron and their customers, Hewlett-Packard and Apple among them, under-stand the importance of powerful but flexible internal planning and control systems.

Although the U.S. market for MRP software lies between $1 billion and $2 billion, MRP designers still overlook purchasing department needs. The old MRP "push" systems model doesn't fit the needs of lean, flexible companies. Many purchasers are frustrated with the purchasing module of their MRP system, for good reason. Most MRP packages tacked purchasing on to the front of the system as an afterthought to keep the paperwork flowing. Included in one consultant's MRP "wish list" are the following points:

- Planning systems should include provisions for "c" class items (nuts and bolts) without volumes of paper transactions.

- Customer MRP systems need to produce separate schedules and backup data that will reduce supplier scheduling costs and speed the supply cycle.
- Customers need supplier rating reports on service, quality performance, delivery (part of service), and price performance. Exception reports and report printouts should come in below the "hernia report level," preferably designed and modified to suit both suppliers and customers.
- Custom features. The system should also capture data by individual team members beyond the usual bill of material, for example, technical notes and performance histories.

The bigger problem with MRP systems is that they were designed years before Just-in-Time took hold. In a JIT environment, MRP should be a *planning*, not an execution, tool. Unfortunately, some companies attempt to use these very complex and transaction-intensive systems to run day-to-day shop floor operations.

How can a company judge when MRP has exceeded its usefulness? It's time to pull the plug when:

- The system drives procurement to produce large discrete batches, but the operation is supposedly a Just-in-Time one.
- There are too many signals, causing planners to spend the first hour of every workday reacting to exception reports. It's like the boy who cried "Wolf!"—sooner or later, people stop listening. If forecast accuracy is 65 percent and manufacturing knows how to cover for the remaining 35 percent, don't use the system to try to "plan away" the difference.
- Procurement and scheduling personnel don't communicate well. The MRP system should be their "Rosetta stone,"[1] not a wall.
- The procurement module becomes "untouchable" because the system accumulates too much data that need to be extracted and sorted into action categories for accurate planning.

- The software can't handle subcontracting. With so many companies "subbing out" manufacturing, it makes sense to use a system that includes good tracking and scheduling features to capture necessary detail.
- The system shows you more than you want to see. Companies with endless product line and options variety will be frustrated by systems that explode every assembly in perfect detail. Planners don't always need to see it all. Some items should be handled offline.

Jimmying MRP

MRP systems don't solve all planning problems. For that reason, users should be selective about MRP. Identify candidates for limited MRP use—products that steadily bump down the line with predictable flow and quality, standardized assemblies that vary only in the trimmings, products made from very available, common components. Use MRP to explode demand estimates and reserve supplier capacities or to aggregate commodity groups for pricing advantage.

Mike Terry, inventory control manager at EMC Corporation of Hopkinton, Massachusetts, which produces mass storage systems and devices, realized that their MRP system represented another opportunity to reduce inventory. Terry did an analysis of a mid-range storage product, looking at major components to see if they really needed to be brought in at the point and in the sequence the system called for. Five components represented 80 percent of the mass storage device's total value: the disk drive, SRAMs, PAL chip, raw board, and the power supply. Looking at system lead times, and thinking about what the optimal number might be for minimum inventory, Terry asked "Could any of these items show up later for the assembly process?" The board and the SRAM could not because they went to Puerto Rico and back. But the subassembly didn't need the disk drive when the MRP signal called for it, ten days before ship date.

Through a subroutine Terry called "negative offset," he tricked the system into asking for the disk drive on Day 5, rather than Day 10. Planners know that this subroutine generated a real signal because a sidebar on the MRP requirement report specifically identifies these special items, showing how many days have been shaved from the system's standard leadtime. All in-ship (inbound inventory expenditures) reporting, which translated into one of management's first inventory dollar targets, future planned orders, reschedule notices, and new procurement requests, key off the new offsets.

The new subroutines allow MRP to reflect new inventory plans more accurately. According to Terry, in-ship projections were constantly massaged prior to the change. This modification, he says, "builds a little more integrity into MRP. We're not doing inventory estimates on the back of a napkin. And we have details and an audit trail in the system." And the new system saved money. Fourteen days cut lead time for only twenty items saved the company $1.7 million in inventory costs.

Procurement organizations that support JIT production should use MRP carefully, not for day-to-day operations but to avoid problems with excess paperwork, high overhead, high inventories and expediting, and purchasing vs. production control conflicts. When used in this way, MRP assumes the role of a powerful long-range capacity and resource planning partner.

3. Procurement Software

The ideal procurement software package should work like the Rosetta stone to integrate all functions across an enterprise, from design through shipping. Most purchasing packages do not quite meet customer needs, frequently being too complex, or allowing little customization by users. Supply management partners, customers and suppliers need a few basic system features, including open order position and quality.

Open order position. Whether a customer places an order with "legal paper" or the business is placed with a handshake, each partner needs to know the numbers—the total quantities and time period agreed upon for delivery (details that would previously have been labeled the "open order file"), and the supplier's actual performance against the open order position. A good supply management system will visually display the performance delivery record so that customers can quickly rate a supplier's service in timeliness and quality.

Quality. MRP systems typically retain some data on scrapped vendor material, or dollars expended for rework. Although that measure is still important, as companies approach zero defects the obvious gross measures become less useful. Instead, quality systems should be an integral part of the supply management system, including relevant certification information, ISO registration status, and customer audit findings, as well as routine quality performance statistics stated numerically and graphically. The objective is to enable a customer to quickly compare the performance of a variety of suppliers without site visits, without redundant audits, and without "trial by fire."

4. Scheduling

Customers need to transmit forecasts for purchased requirements to their supplier. In more advanced partnerships, suppliers download the production plan directly from the customer's system. Ideally, the schedule horizon extends far enough to cover lead times and to allow the supplier to order raw materials.

A reverse scheduling sequence is now possible. The supplier can transmit directly to the customer's production facility weekly schedules derived from earlier customer input of rough requirements. With this approach, the supplier must have reached a high and very predictable quality level; his delivery performance must be equally consistent.

Contract Manufacturing Scheduling Issues

Subcontracting, or contract manufacturing, is neglected in most scheduling packages, so many purchasers have established manual subsystems to compensate for the system's lack of detail. A JIT supply manager needs two pieces of information on parts handled by contractors: their production/delivery schedule, and the inventory balances on raw material stored at the subcontractor site. That inventory belongs in the customer's inventory account, even if it is shipped directly from the source to the contractor. Because some but not all requirements for a particular part may be supplied by the contractor, the inventory control module of the system should maintain that data by stockroom location.

5. Networking Communications Utilities

In global sourcing networks, where materials pass from international suppliers through U.S. customs into a local network, hand-offs take time and create quality problems. One of the solutions intended to simplify transportation is EDI (Electronic Data Interchange). Although EDI has come to mean data transfer, "network communications" is a more appropriate term that better defines application. Network utilities are essential to track inbound materials where the pipeline supports JIT production schedules. Networking is also important at the customer end of the system, where suppliers or purchasers need to monitor outbound shipments in great detail.

JIT inventory levels can be maintained at low levels only if the pipeline is supported by excellent communications systems. Dr. Yossi Sheffi, director of the MIT Center for Transportation, believes that good information systems can essentially replace warehouses. Through these systems many carriers will be able to provide detailed views of material moving through thousands of depots and terminals in the pipeline, the kind of detailed information that is essential for JIT customers dependent on suppliers a world away.[2]

The best JIT and post-JIT/TQM systems also offer reduced transport costs with better control of freight/truck scheduling. Transportation, especially premium service for tracking, expediting, etc., costs money. (In 1990, total logistics costs in the United States were approximately $545 billion, or 10.5 percent of the GNP![3]) JIT supply management must include all transportation details, from information tracking and paperwork functions associated with it, to bill of lading generation and freight bill payments.

A South Carolina minimill steel plant manager, a self-described "victim of JIT," felt that his JIT customers required him to carry more inventory, in greater variety, than he would like, certainly greater volume than his financial instincts would approve. His reason for carrying the extra inventory was the challenge of truck scheduling. The mill is located in a remote area where delivery problems get worse during watermelon season. The transportation manager frets about daily shipping schedules. She has found it almost impossible to compete for the services of small truckers with melon farmers eager to send their $.10 per pound produce to Northern $.50-per-pound markets. The company has been forced to switch from cheaper, independent truckers to bigger, more expensive fleets with available trucks and excellent scheduling/tracking systems.

Some organizations, like Bose, dedicate considerable internal resources to inbound freight control. Indeed, where manufacturing is not world-class in speed, quality, or flexibility, excellent inbound shipment tracking can compensate for scheduling weaknesses, and thus keep very demanding customers satisfied.

Paul Tagliamonte, Bose's transportation system guru, contrasts the old multistep manual tracking process with Bose's streamlined flows, starting with the following eight-step scenario:

"THE OLD WAY"

1. Customer calls inquiring about shipment status.

2. Sales representative takes the customer's purchase order number, promising to get back to him shortly.

3. Sales representative accesses customer p.o. number in supplier's order processing system, then cross-references it to an order number.

4. Sales rep contacts logistics department for a tracer.

5. Logistics administrator promises to supply tracer data soon. Clerk researches the bill of lading file looking for actual ship date, bill of lading number, carrier name, number of pieces, and weight.

6. Logistics administrator phones carrier requesting shipment status.

7. Carrier representative takes information, promising to phone back with answer.

8. Carrier returns call with information that is transferred to Logistics, then to Sales, and finally to the customer.

This scenario is a waste of time. The supplier must maintain a legion of clerks, much like pre-JIT production expediters, to fill in the pieces of the puzzle, and customers inevitably lose interest in the supplier.

Bose's transportation and logistics systems were upgraded to simplify the eight-step process and to give the customer greater immediate access to shipping data. The company automated bill of lading creation, and Bose logistics managers and customs personnel can dial directly into shippers' systems to follow shipments. The system accumulates and graphically displays comparative quality performance among various transportation suppliers, in total and at the individual terminal level, a quality feature that pinpoints problems as they arise. Tracing performed by various shipping personnel clerks by phone and with manually acquired data has been replaced with a system keyed to either bill of lading or p.o. number, ship date, store number, or department number. Finally, freight bills are paid by wire. After the system cross-checks receipts against purchase orders, the company's bank is authorized by modem to transfer funds to pay shippers' bills.[4]

THE SYSTEMS CHALLENGE

Systems integration is the next challenge. Within three to five years most customer and supplier organizations will easily "talk" across modems, exchanging schedule and forecast data, as well as detailed design specifications. In addition, good, simple systems for successful partners will be designed to satisfy other internal needs beyond basic data exchange. Procurement systems must connect to design and production departments as well as to MRP systems so that designers can easily access purchasing and capital equipment "notes."

The final and more important challenge is to use systems to drastically cut time and the number of steps necessary to move from a concept design to full production. Here, systems integration is a software issue to be addressed after users have answered the basic process question: Which steps in the current process must be retained and performed by software? The answer is to simplify, to reduce time and steps *before* the software is installed. Fewer loops mean better information, reducing the number of "intellectual setups."

We're almost there. The next—and more challenging—partnering development area, people systems, is dependent on good communications tools. Companies that provide their people with fully integrated, simple systems will have the advantage over those enterprises that address only one segment of human systems, say, teams or compensation.

NOTES

1. The Rosetta stone is a tablet, discovered by one of Napoleon's soldiers in Egypt, that unlocked the meaning of Egyptian hieroglyphs. Because the stone carried the same text in Egyptian hieroglyphics, Greek, and demotic characters, once scholars had understood the Greek and demotic, they eventually were able to decipher the hieroglyphics as well.

2. Peter Bradley, "The World in a Computer Window," *Purchasing*, July 16, 1992, p. 52.

3. Robert Millen, "JIT Logistics: Putting JIT on Wheels," *Target*, Summer 1991, pp. 4–12.

4. Paul C. Tagliamonte, "The Successful Implementation of EDI at Bose Corporation," July 1992.

CHAPTER 7

Partnering People Systems

The only means of competition left will be human assets.
Lester Thurow, Dean, MIT's Sloan School of Management

In breakthrough partnerships, a new work-force development approach is essential. It is not possible to prepare people, design curricula, and develop training programs without a vision of the future workplace. Motorola, Xerox, IBM, and other big first-tier companies have long-established, rich training and development programs, and smaller companies can learn much from these pioneers.

Let's look at the manufacturing planning world of twenty years ago, traces of which remain as barriers to strong partnerships. We're in a material planning department where I learned the basics of MRP and master scheduling—although, typically, this department did everything *but* material planning or master scheduling. The company was Digital Equipment Corporation in happier times. Although planners and schedulers at DEC had a few basic planning tools, the way work really got done was through politics, a.k.a. horsetrading ("I've got one tape drive I'll trade for your line printer") and brute-force number crunching.

Every quarter all the materials folks gathered up hundreds of 2″ × 6″ planning slips—actual bill of material explosions—and headed down the road to the Old Mill Restaurant to grind out next quarter's forecast. And every end-of-month we *all* got to drive forktrucks of computers down to shipping.

After all the numbers were entered and massaged, or padded "just-in-case," and a few beers consumed, we returned to the plant to play out the mystery of the planning cycle. And mysterious it was! A full MRP requirements planning sheet as we now know it would include on-hand (warehouse) information, safety stock calculations, and other background data. But at Digital in 1973 most of that data was in the heads of a few impressive planners, because, as the saying went, "We make computers, we don't use them."

Like the parts list on a new car, computers have thousands of components originating with dozens of suppliers. A buyer or production planner faced with the complexity of building an evolving product, besieged with engineering change orders, needed a strong constitution.

The toughest of this ilk was Joe Bradford, three hundred pounds of cigar-smoking human cpu power. Joe could recite a PDP8 bill of materials at twenty yards. Renowned throughout the distribution community, he could expedite anything. Single-source rare parts appeared on his desk overnight. When negotiations for a critical part failed, Joe had other ways to make you say yes.

Joe's description of his ideal materials/purchasing person was pretty narrow. He needed someone who liked long stints working with numbers, interrupted by daily production panics. College degrees or special outside training courses were not encouraged. But the ability to consume quarts of beer was helpful, to drink off the stress. Joe and his crew were fond of late nights at the Veterans of Foreign Wars hall and an occasional celebratory Saturday-morning beer bust as the final shipment wheeled down to the dock.

PERSONAL VS. ELECTRONIC NETWORKS

Joe's quite a contrast to the planners of twenty years later, many of whom have been renamed "supply managers." He has been replaced with a white-shirted female MBA, looking to earn her stripes in the trenches. On her desk sit all the tools computer scheduling and planning systems designers can offer, from user-friendly material planning detail and summary sheets to software networks that access supplier's, even trucker's, schedules and forecasts.

WHAT'S REALLY CHANGING?

While Joe's world was built on personal networking and the ability to "save the day" when numbers couldn't, his replacement has at her fingertips more information than she can use through electronic networking. Have we reached the long-predicted Age of the Knowledge-based Worker? The proliferation of PC's says it's here, but all the computer tools and power did not solve the classic forecasting or scheduling problems—they simply become clearer, sooner. Joe's replacement has a different title, different skills, and is a master at the PC keyboard.

How did we come this far, and what's next? Five major changes have happened on the way from Joe to his replacement:

1. *Competition.* DEC's playing field narrowed as other younger competitors came on: first, prodigal son Data General, followed by Prime, Apollo (now Hewlett-Packard), Sun, and numerous others.

2. *Computer planning systems.* Commercial MRP and other planning packages are cheap and user-friendly. Joe's first "modern" computer tool, a re-creation of IBM's RPS (Requirements

Planning System), was assembled in off-hours by a production technician. It shaved a few hours off the Old Mill forecasting sessions, but without inventory balances and pegged requirements, it was only a simple explosion program that gave users an incomplete picture of a component position.

3. *JIT.* On Joe's production floor, components accumulated in dozens of small feeder stockrooms, all guarded well by his personal minions. In a separate building, equal in size to the production facility, Joe erected a multi-million-dollar, fully automated warehouse (except when the robot let a nine hundred–pound disk drive slip between its fingers from five shelves up!). The epitome of accumulated inventory decisions—"just-in-case," rework, and hundreds of unaccounted-for last-minute schedule changes—the warehouse filled within hours of its dedication.

JIT of course requires that all waste disappear, including accumulations of unused materials. So from this twenty-year distance the only benefit we can find in Joe's edifice is that, for the first time in his facility's history, all bits and pieces of good and bad forecasting, all negotiating chips in the form of disk drives and cables and connectors and monitors surfaced in one central area—visual management made real.

4. *Quality.* Integration of outsourced materials, improved component quality, and therefore predictability, cut into Joe's empire. Taking inventories from one turn up to six reduced his power base: less trading, fewer allocation squabbles, empty shelves in the warehouse, stilled forklift trucks at the receiving dock. As quality continued its climb, planning and purchasing folks could look ahead more. Systems that may have sat three weeks in assembly awaiting inspection while diagnostics were run were replaced by onsite integration and the assembly of major components at the customer's site. As component reliability got closer to 100 per-

cent, computer manufacturers did not need to debug, run, and test systems for weeks in the factory. Systems were integrated at customer site, and they would run well (usually) the first time you powered up.

5. *Work force shifts*. Back in 1973 one or two DEC plant people held college degrees (they were well hidden.) But by the late seventies various groups and professional societies were starting to encroach on Joe's territory.

The appearance of each newcomer upped the ante on professional skills. Although early APICS chapter meetings frequently resembled "boys' night out," attendees' enthusiastic acceptance of new planning techniques and certification exams contributed to generally lifting professional skills and credibility.

First were the National Association of Purchasing Managers (NAPM) and American Production and Inventory Control Society (APICS), followed by APICS spinoff AME (Association for Manufacturing Excellence). Women and minorities became features on the landscape, and although their entry in the work force may have been unwelcome, by sheer numbers they diversified the image of the new material planning professional.

The purchasing environment of twenty years ago has acquired a new name, new systems, and new professional credentials. Purchasing as a very narrow function that worked with other narrow functions—materials planning, quality, production control—has been replaced with procurement and supply management organizations, many of which are team-based. Planning professionals in supply management have mastered new technical skills; next, they need to acquire the mature partnering skills that their seamless and wall-less environment requires. That means moving along the partnering path and perfecting the Seven Breakthrough Partnering Drivers—to reiterate:

1. Quality
2. Timeliness
3. Excellent communications
4. Flexibility
5. The attitude of continuous improvement
6. The habit of collaboration
7. Trust

The first two elements, quality and timeliness, are basic requirements to perform JIT. Perfecting quality systems—planning, measurement, and control—requires organizationwide acceptance and day-to-day use of the basic quality tools: Pareto, scatter diagrams, and Fishbone (discussed in detail in Chapter 9, "Quality Basics").

Timeliness, the second basic requirement of JIT, means that external and internal suppliers must deliver product when and in the correct sequence to support customer operations. Honda's suppliers understand that even if their production schedules are not synchronous with their customer's, their deliveries must be.

Training people like Joe to excel at the Seven Breakthrough Partnering Drivers is a lifetime challenge, well beyond the boundaries of typical culture change. People need a safe opportunity to learn and try out new ideas, then practice them in an environment that welcomes improvement. The DEC of twenty years ago, growing at 100 percent per year, had little time for the exploration of improvements beyond what it took to get today's shipment down to the dock. Now, however, all sides of a partnership agreement—customer procurement personnel, and supplier production and marketing/customer service people—must be highly skilled in two key areas, communications and quality. They should master the JIT basics, have the urge to continuously analyze and improve performance, and be team players.

Companies don't need to reinvent curricula each time a company or small work team starts an improvement program. A few others have gone down this path before, and even though the journey won't be the same, the predecessors' experience is invaluable.

EXCELLENCE MODELS

In 1987, well before Motorola won the Baldrige Award, the company started Motorola University. By 1991 the company had delivered 123,000 hours of training through licensing, and in 1991, 6,500 individuals participated in courses offered there. CEO Galvin recognized that to reach the company's very ambitious Six Sigma quality goal (fewer than 3.4 defects per million), suppliers must also have Six Sigma capability.

At first, Motorola U. offered three courses: "Design for Manufacturability," "Statistical Process Control" (one-day course), and "Manufacturing Cycle Management" (JIT).

The program expanded after it opened, in 1987, to suppliers, who were charged the same fee as internal customers, $150 per day. Nineteen-ninety saw the addition of "Understanding Six Sigma," which focused on quality methods applied to administrative business functions like purchasing and order administration. Motorola's investment in all training totals $150 million, an impressive figure. In 1992, 3.34 percent of payroll was spent on training, up from the previous year's 2.9 percent. In addition, Motorola has joined with seven other companies (Digital, Xerox, Sematech, TI, Kodak, Texaco, and Chrysler) in a Consortium for Supplier Training (CST), a consortium that is designed to take portions of Motorola University's curriculum and offer them at reasonable rates through selected community colleges, and other educational groups, to small suppliers and customers.

Preferred Suppliers Program

As the company expanded its training programs, Motorola trimmed its supply base and started a Preferred Suppliers program. The objective was to shrink its supply base and only buy from suppliers who met high quality and delivery standards.

Obviously, the shift from 4,200 suppliers in 1985 to 25 percent of that number by 1992 caused fierce competition among Motorola's suppliers. The winners continue to meet their customer's quality and delivery requirements. Their success is in large part due to work-force training.

Core curriculum

Four courses have become standard requirements across the corporation: Six Sigma, Design for Manufacturability, Manufacturing Cycle Management, and SPC for Process Quality Improvement. Preferred Suppliers must have completed these core requirements, which Motorola's Supply Management Council mandates as basic certification requirements. Of the over 200 courses, "Design for Manufacturability" is the most popular.

By the end of 1992 the company had delivered through licensing 125,000 hours of training. Approximately 100,000 workers have taken the Six Sigma course alone. Course delivery sites are worldwide, supporting the global supplier network. Human capital is a resource to be nurtured long-term, like any other capital investment. Motorola employees must undertake a minimum of five days training per year.

TABLE 7.1: Motorola Supply Base

	TOTAL SUPPLIERS	PREFERRED SUPPLIERS
1992	1,085	324 ($3.2 billion)
1990	1,158	333
1989	1,238	383
1987	1,800	600
1986	2,100	800
1985	4,200	0

Source: Paul Brault, Worldwide Director for Customer and Supplier Training, Motorola

FIGURE 7.1: Motorola University Offerings

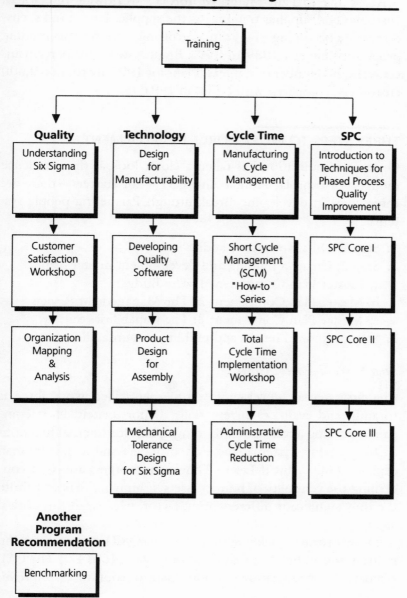

According to Paul Brault, Motorola's worldwide director of customer and supplier training, as the supplier base shrinks, customers are becoming a bigger and growing section of the training program. Between 1989 to 1991 Brault saw a 600 percent increase in the number of trainees. Plans for 1993 are to train 9,000 customers, compared with 6,500 in 1991.

THREE STEPS TO WORK-FORCE DEVELOPMENT

Once an organization has taken a closer look at the excellence models—Motorola, Honda, and CST,℠ for starters—there are three steps in developing Breakthrough Partnering people systems:

1. Step 1: Do a work-force audit.
2. Step 2: Create a training and development master plan.
   a. Master Plan Component 1: The Budget
   b. Master Plan Component 2: The Management Review
   c. Master Plan Component 3: The Capabilities Survey
3. Step 3: Reward results and build in accountability.

Step 1: Work-Force Audit

The first step in developing a superbly skilled work force is to audit and evaluate current skills. Unfortunately, most companies develop audits and long-range plans for internal functions such as quality, systems, and new products and avoid "human capital" audits. But if Lester Thurow and others are right concerning the centrality of human assets, if human assets constitute the only significant differentiating factor, why avoid this critical area?

The Motorola Quality System Review (QSR) is a good starting point in the audit. (See figure 7.2 on pages 146–147.) The QSR evaluates an organization's commitment to continuous improvement through training and development in several areas as well as other quality improvement topics. The self-scoring questions in the QSR allow organizations to identify their areas and levels of competence. In Subsection 1.8, for example, a score of "poor," no training plan, implies that the company is really not in the game; "outstanding," a rating that few companies achieve, implies complete management support, mature deployment, and superior results.

The audit has ten subsections in all, and can be self-administered. The scoring elements are arranged so that test takers will see a progression from no activity to outstanding performance, in both deployment and results. Although the Motorola assessment system is not a complete guide for customer/supplier organizations, it gives a full picture of how one Baldrige award winner continues to develop quality commitment.

Step 2: Training and Development Master Plan

Every organization needs a master plan. Although it is easy to skip the detailed thinking required to develop a plan that will take an organization into its next stage of development, without one human resource development is haphazard and wasteful. Companies may spend thousands of training dollars ineffectively. A Midwestern pump manufacturer spent $6 million in eight months to train its entire organization in Total Quality, but six months after training, no one in the organization was using the new tools. The money was wasted because the organization wasn't ready to let people use their new skills.

The primary objective in delivering an effective long-term training and organizational plan is to ensure that all activities are consistent, integrated, reinforced, and truly reflective of the organization's short- and long-term business needs. The master plan includes modules that map out how the organization will develop in three key areas:

1. *Training.* A short-term solution to strengthen specific skill-related areas (e.g., CAD training, sales skills, product training) for *immediate* job application.
2. *Development.* A longer-term solution to strengthen the total individual or identified group to meet future business needs (e.g., a degree, a mentor program, a series of training programs, and on-the-job practice).
3. *Organizational development.* Short- and long-term solutions to help the organization manage cultural change efforts on all levels (e.g., team building, organizational structuring, succession planning, enhancing group productivity).

The master plan for organizational development is the project plan package that guides human resource development through each operating step. The package contains three component modules, each with specific details: Component 1, the Budget (the cost of development); Component 2, the Management Review (evaluation of the organization's current skills); Component 3, Capabilities Survey (a detailed examination of management's development priorities and needs compared with the current skill sets).

Master Plan Component 1: The Budget

There are several ways to arrive at a budget for training and development. Some organizations calculate dollars or hours of training per employee. Others need to consider the breakdown of these dollars because there is a price difference between outside seminars (from colleges, universities, and consulting/training houses) and internal training (outside contractors on-site, or a do-it-yourself "train the trainers" approach). The easiest approach is simply to factor a growth percentage into current budgets and project forward.

If your group is contemplating major cultural changes, however, benchmark before budgeting and developing the master plan. Find out what your competitors are doing and spend more wisely, or look at Motorola and other models of excellence for specific curriculum guidelines.

Industry standards should be part of the benchmark file. Some industry data is available from The American Society for Training and Development (ASTD, in Alexandria, Virginia), a good source of training help and planning data.

Master Plan Component 2: The Management Review

Early on, administration of the QSR questions identifies weak areas in an organization that should be more closely examined. One follow-up approach is to conduct individual focused interviews that evaluate workers' skills and identify their personal development goals.

A different approach was taken by a small high-tech start-up struggling with growth. The human resources manager conducted thirty-five individual interviews with senior and mid-level managers, accompanied by seven focus groups of first-line managers and supervisors from the same functional areas. This group approach allowed the researcher to establish training priorities for specific functions, e.g., purchasing, engineering, production. A managers' "wish list" emerged from the interviews:

1. General management skills
2. Business information
3. Continuous improvement skills
4. Communications skills
5. PC training
6. New hire training/orientation
7. Sales training
8. Project managment skills

For an organization with limited resources but specific market-driven requirements, enabling specific functions to leapfrog old practices with large doses of practical training works well. A

FIGURE 7.2 Excerpts on Training and Development from Motorola Quality System Review (QSR)

Subsection 1.8, Quality System Management, asks:

Is management's support of ongoing training (including quality training) sufficient and is it documented by an organizational training plan?

Poor: No training plan exists. There is no management support for developing one.

Weak: Some training is performed as time and budget allow. There is no documented training plan. Some managers recognize the need for business/quality training.

Fair: A formal training system exists within the organization. Training tends to be limited primarily to manufacturing related skills. Training for new hires and transfers exists in some areas of the business. There is general awareness of the need for quality training by management.

Marginally Qualified: Annual training plans for the whole organization are required by management. Most employees receive some job related training. Training plans generally tie to business and quality objectives. The training plan is fully documented and includes all new hires, transfers, and managers.

Qualified: All employees have received comprehensive training that recognizes individual needs and development. Training plans and progress are reviewed regularly by all levels of management. Measures have been established to evaluate training effectiveness in support of strategic plans.

Outstanding: Training at all levels is driven by strategic objectives and individual development needs and is aligned with customer satisfaction requirements and expectations. Training effectiveness measures clearly demonstrate a positive impact of training in accomplishing business and customer satisfaction results.

Subsection 6.1, Problem Solving Techniques.

Are enough people adequately trained in problem solving techniques in comparison to the needs of the organization, such as: stratification, check sheet, histogram, Pareto diagram, cause and effect analysis, scatter diagram, and control charts, Design of Experiments (DOE), advanced problem-solving techniques, team oriented problem solving, Taguchi Methods, Design for Manufacturability, etc.

Subsection 8.1 Human Resources Involvement.

Does management ensure that all personnel are fully familiar with their role in achieving total customer satisfaction?

8.2 Do all personnel know how their performance impacts internal and external customer satisfaction?

8.3 Can all personnel who contact external customers properly reflect quality improvement programs (such as Six Sigma)?

8.4 Are sufficient personnel participating in professional societies and growth programs?

8.5 Are all personnel trained in sufficient detail to support key initiatives?

8.6 Are the results of training properly evaluated and indicated program changes made?

8.7 Does a policy exist which encourages the cross training and rotation of personnel, and is this policy used as the basis of job progression?

8.8 Are proper performance standards (including customer satisfaction standards) participatively developed and regularly applied to all personnel?

8.9 Are total customer satisfaction programs and resulting successes publicized to all personnel?

8.10 Do goal setting and reward/incentive programs properly support the quality improvement process?

Reprinted from "Workforce Development," Patricia E. Moody, *Target*, February, 1993.

synergy occurs when co-workers from the same department learn and experiment with new practices.

Master Plan Component 3: The Capabilities Survey

Various survey instruments address culture and training/development issues. To guarantee that training resources develop the high-priority areas identified, some companies use a capabilities survey. This instrument compares current skill strengths with management priorities. The goal is to identify mismatches that require development.

For example, if management rates "being a team leader" as of "high importance," but employees evaluate the company's relative strength in teams as "very weak," the task is clear. For the top three or four capabilities that require strengthening, the organization can then locate or design training to fill the need. In the electronics start-up described earlier, the profile results required ongoing customer/supplier training.

Step 3: Reward Results, Build In Accountability

Training without accountability is wasted time and money. Although the U.S. educational system has experimented with numerous pass/fail options, American industry doesn't have the luxury of getting a "pass" grade on quality when competitors can produce with "no defects." Shouldn't the goals of a training program be as specific as a full school grading system? There is a great danger that many institutions, seeing a decline in the eighteen- to twenty-four-year-old population, will seize on adult education and retraining as their new market, without the report cards that guarantee customer satisfaction. It's easy to see how education and training needs have lost their alignment with administrative and budget issues. Training without accountability— tests without grades, or pass/fail—isn't good enough for the customer.

TABLE 7.2: Corporate Capabilities Profile Summary

The following capabilities were reported as having the highest importance with the lowest current relative strength.

MANAGEMENT LEVEL	CAPABILITY	TRAINING TRACKS FOR FUTURE PROGRAMS
Senior managers	Build customer-supplier alliances Manage innovation	1. Corporate performance values: Includes problem solving, creative thinking, building customer/supplier sensitivity, data analysis, facilitating groups, active listening and communication skills, and working in teams.
Middle managers	Build customer-supplier alliances Develop and coach others	2. Business information: Product information, policies and procedures, MRP. 3. Business knowledge: Financial and project management, strategic planning, employee selection.
First-line managers/ supervisors	Communicate effectively Develop and coach others	4. Technical/functional knowledge: Programming languages, material planning, accounting. 5. Interpersonal skills: Performance evaluation, being a coach, listening and giving feedback. 6. Personal development: Writing and presentation skills, time management, stress management.

A wonderful example of how a company can reward serious employee dedication to learning new technologies comes from Molex, an Illinois connector producer. The connector industry continues to become more competitive, staying ahead requires extremely high quality, superior design skills, as well as a global presence. Molex is to a large extent owned and managed by the Krehbiel family; three generations of the family currently work there. Each family member has "paid his dues," preparing for management by learning several job functions, and getting to know as many of the employees as possible. Even though the company is approaching the half-billion-dollar mark, it still has the feeling of a small company.

An indication of Molex management's dedication to helping employees grow and to retaining the small company environment is special attention to training and development. For example, students who complete a rigorous five-week advanced statistics course are hosted at an awards luncheon. President John Krehbiel, Jr., presents each student with ten shares of company stock, a true investment in human capital.

WHAT'S GOOD FOR THE FIRST TIER IS NOT NECESSARILY GOOD FOR THE SECOND

What happens to second-tier producers, suppliers to the excellence models like Motorola and Xerox? Is the journey to excellence the same for them?

The answer is no. For example, it is unrealistic and deceptive to expect one of Honda's suppliers to replicate the Marysville facility, mirroring organization structures, measurement and control systems, and work-force training. Honda needs suppliers that can, at a minimum, predictably and consistently meet quality and delivery standards, the first two Breakthrough Partnering Drivers. Small suppliers, because of their size and position further upstream, do not have the same production issues as their downstream customers. For example, a supplier of plastic instrument panel parts to an auto assembly plant is working not only with different technologies and technical problems but also with different environmental, process, and work-force issues.

The work force at a first-tier supplier usually earns significantly more than that of most second-tier suppliers. As GM has learned, assembly labor averages $15 to $25 per hour, plus extensive health and other benefit costs, whereas at their second-tier suppliers, many of whom will be taking the hit for big cost reductions, wages fall into the $8- to $15-per-hour range.

The Consortium Approach to Work-Force Development

One approach to small supplier work force development lies in pooling resources so that small and mid-size companies have access to wider training choices, while sharing the expense. A good example of this approach is SEMATECH, a technology consortium headquartered in Texas that was formed when thirteen first-tier firms pooled financial resources with the support of government funding. Although continued funding is uncertain, the consortium has produced some valuable training aids in the quality area.

A few SEMATECH members, including Digital Equipment Corporation, Motorola, and Texas Instruments have formed an educational group, called The Consortium for Supplier Training,™ geared to offering courses aimed at smaller suppliers through the community college system. The educational consortium is reviewing plans to locate training centers in various spots across the United States. Two New England centers have been agreed upon, and plans are to have seven in place by the end of 1993, each offering four Motorola licensed courses. Motorola's Paul Brault feels that community colleges provide a good match with the consortium's mission because most suppliers are located within fifty miles of a community college, of which there are 1,222 in the United States.

As further proof of its commitment, in February 1992, The Consortium met with a group of eighteen leading community colleges called the League for Innovation. The Consortium challenged the college leaders to practice TQM within their own walls, and the colleges responded by starting to provide TQM training to administrators and professors.

The Consortium is totally nonprofit, and no dues are exacted. Instead, the unusual price of admission to the consortium is that a company must sponsor a college. Digital, for example, plans to sponsor a community college in Boston. Pairing industry leaders with educators guarantees the accountability of program design; curriculum delivery must support industry needs.

Almost every college and company contacted about CST has a positive response: "Where do we sign?" One limitation on sudden expansion is that each college must have a corporate sponsor, and an advisory board will manage expansion of the program. The organization will perform quality audits of training delivery and course quality over time.

Why would Motorola share its courses with colleges? According to Mr. Brault, "If Motorola can get five hundred community colleges teaching best-in-practice skills to the supply base, we'll raise the quality level of this country overnight." The added benefit, of course, is that this education collaboration fosters cooperation among corporations.

Any company that gets involved with the Baldrige Awards knows that there are many sections in the criteria that focus on what companies are doing with suppliers. When companies start educating suppliers on one level, they will want to progress to the next. Brault summarizes the consortium strategy: "It doesn't take a rocket scientist to understand that as you start improving quality, you need fewer suppliers, and those have to be very good. And where do they get the materials to be very good? We want to give them the materials to improve."

CST's approach views the established college systems as a distribution channel. The group also helps standardize quality instruction across various companies. The intent is also to limit the number of different quality audits customers impose on their suppliers.

CST members developed a three-step process to standardize the facility certification process. The instructor/candidate must 1) attend the class sponsored by the course owner; 2) complete train-the-trainer course offered by the course owner, and 3) co-teach (or co-facilitate) with the Master Instructor from the course owner company. There are a few conditions of participation: The college must identify an instructor who will be the designated trainer and who will go through the certification process. Should the trainer fail the certification test, he or she can try again.

Honda

Honda of America has also developed training resources that are routinely shared with suppliers. In addition to full training sessions, Honda offers suppliers the opportunity to receive training on special issues such as the Disabilities Act and various EPA regulatory practices.

Dave Nelson, Honda of America's vice president of purchasing, describes his approach to supplier evaluation and development: "Every one is different. You need to look at suppliers that you develop on a case-by-case basis to understand their greatest needs, their strengths and weaknesses."

Nypro

Nypro is a $150 million-per-year Massachusetts plastics producer that has found a strategy to leverage its very aggressive training and development activities by partnering with various expert training sources. Nypro Institute, located in a restored eighteenth-century carpet mill in Clinton, Massachusetts, started fourteen years ago as a small training program. It evolved into offering noncredit and college credit courses leading to associate's and MBA degrees. Their Certificate in Plastics Technology includes courses in the company's "bread and butter" activities: injection molding, mold design, polymeric materials, blueprint reading, hydraulics and pneumatics, industrial electrical maintenance, SPC (statistical process control), and principles of supervision.

Course participation is about equally divided between company insiders and outsiders—customers, suppliers, even competitors, most of whom are small regional molders. Outsiders pay $225 per course. (The institute runs as a cost center, not for profit.) During one semester over 500 students were enrolled in Nypro Institute and 120 participated in the certification program. The institute delivered a total of 10,000 hours of training, all without the "carrot" of company incentive programs.

Paul Jensen, Nypro corporate director of training and development, describes the program as "highly leveraged." Paul is the only full-time trainer, and the institute draws on faculty resources from nearby educational institutions to supplement in-house professionals doubling as trainers. The plastics certificate program partners with Fitchburg State College, plastics seminars are shared with the University of Lowell, computer classes are under the auspices of Catapult, a training house. Associate's degree courses may be taught by professors from Mount Wachusett Community College. The new MBA program is partnered with full-time professors from Worcester Polytechnic Institute, where Nypro President Gordon Lankton is a member of the board of directors. According to Jensen, forming alliances with academic and training houses "provides lots of different topics with low staff. We will never have a big training department."

Expanding the program into the twelve other plant sites is

the next challenge for Jensen. He plans to use computer-based interactive training, and video conferencing to the other facilities.

"Certified Workers"

Other second-tier development efforts are springing up across the country. One of the most intriguing visions of work-force development popped up in a full-page *Industry Week* ad pitching Virginia as a place where employees "speak TQM and ISO 9000." Clearly aimed at Northern companies considering relocation, the availability of trained and "quality-literate" workers is presented as a very attractive alternative for companies struggling with education problems and union-management issues. Imagine a prospective industrial park developer sitting down with local government and real estate executives to review the start-up package—but this is what is happening. The agenda includes taxes and tax incentives, highway and airport location, *and the number of certified workers available per functional category.*

In the past, American companies ran apprenticeship programs for employees such as machinists and welders. Industry participated fully in the programs, classifications were standardized, and employers knew what they were hiring. Although restructuring of the machine tool industry has reduced the number of highly skilled machinists, the need for well-trained people with clearly described work skills has not evaporated. The requirements have become more complex and simpler at the same time. Employers require more complex technical skills with, say, computer design systems, but simpler basic performance requirements like English-language competency and on-the-job literacy.

One of the accountability goals of work-force training and development programs should be a standardized system of worker certification. The program may be as simple as a checklist certifying that the worker has completed a series of courses designed by Motorola to develop competency in basic statistical control. Or, going beyond the checklist of completed courses, the program could be a combination of completed exams, mentoring, and internships. Without this very deliberate approach to work-force development the United States will continue to operate with a hodgepodge of internal and external training assessments, and uneven functional skill levels.

THE WRONG ROAD TO WORK-FORCE DEVELOPMENT

The hardest thing is to give money away.
Dave Nelson

Money helps but it doesn't provide all the answers. Recently, a group of large and small companies in the New England region was invited to a three-day conference to explore how they could collaborate with various state and federal government groups to help small suppliers. The government has large sums money to use for helping small second- and third-tier companies, and the questions include how to use the funds, who should administer their use, how to identify the courses that suppliers actually need, and how to determine the amount of time employees can commit to training.

The original conference was well-intentioned but flawed, with the result that industry practitioners, particularly supplier representatives, dropped out, and now consultants and trainers are filling their seats. The net result? Millions of training dollars will get spent no matter who attends the meetings, but course offerings won't reflect the needs of small suppliers or their large customers. Government administrators support what they can understand and what is publicly acceptable—which typically translates into training courses on "competitiveness" and "Total Quality."

Government has a hard time hearing industry, not because well-intentioned administrators are ignorant bureaucrats, but because industry is not speaking with a clear, united voice. Big customers and their supplier networks must become education and workforce development leaders. They need to define how government and educational institutions can help industry reach competitive goals, whether a company wants to reach Six Sigma, or apply for the Baldrige Award, or prepare for ISO 9000 registration.

Government alone is not the answer to small business's need for certified workers. Can academia help? You guessed the answer: No. Unfortunately, academics are still not rewarded for taking sabbaticals in real-world industry. Their research bases often build on literature searches rather than stints on the assembly-line or in the boardroom. ("Banana Time," a rare example of an organizational behavior case study written by an assembly line worker turned professor, is an exception.) The answer to the questions of establishing certification criteria and preparing employees to fulfill them has to come from industry, driven by customers, and supported by like-minded improvement consortia.

INDUSTRY TALKS TO ACADEME

Two years ago Richard Cole, the chairman of Lytron, a Massachusetts producer of heat exchangers, and also a member of the corporation of Wentworth Institute in Boston, decided to do something about the shortcomings he saw in engineering and manufacturing job applicants. Cole felt that "young people do not perceive the career opportunities in manufacturing as being attractive and many of those that do are not adequately prepared."

Cole talked with industry colleagues, and the consensus was that newly minted graduates generally were weak in engineering fundamentals: basic technical understanding and the ability to assimilate new problems quickly. Although new graduates might have learned computer-aided design, they lacked the insight that comes from more traditional drafting experience. And there was universal concern over poor communications skills: writing, speaking, and drawing. The existing approach to hands-on experience and classwork wasn't doing the job.

Cole felt that the problem wasn't unique to Wentworth graduates, but that "as a general standards deterioration issue, we are slipping. Standards come up again and again. There has been a general deterioration in quality—quality of secondary school . . . preparation, quality of program applicants, and a lack of critical standards for the engineering programs."

A contributor to the problem seemed to be that schools feel compelled to offer more and more specialized courses. Offerings have increased, but the school year and the length of the class hour have not. Cole's observations from Lytron led him to recognize the need to educate specifically for careers in manufacturing: "We need more hands-on engineers, a curriculum with lots of time in the labs and shop. Yet it also needs to be grounded in basic fundamentals and science."

Meeting first with the president of Wentworth, Cole asked to "do something for the school." They talked about the problem, formed a committee, developed new courses, and started a program of curriculum reform that resulted in a new four-year manufacturing degree program.

Wentworth President John Van Domelen agreed with Cole's assessment of the educational gaps. "One of the real problems in the United States is that engineering has fundamentally abandoned the manufacturing areas. The fit between the theoretical engineer that is being graduated and the type of job that is necessary on the production floor is not good. There has to be a practical application in the reality of the workplace and it just has not been there before."

Cole's and Wentworth's program is revolutionary. Cole's recommendations for a revised educational program included:

1. *Raise academic standards.* Recruit heavily and offer significant financial aid so that no qualified applicants will choose not to enroll because of costs.
2. *Curriculum review.* Assess the curriculum with an eye toward broad revisions, preparing for "lifelong learning" in science, physics, chemistry, math, communications, drafting and drawing, and manufacturing processes.
3. *"Enlightened self-interest."* In addition to a faculty advisor, every freshman student has an *industrial mentor*, a senior manager of a company who works with the student for four years, providing guidance on course selection, summer jobs, coop programs, and placement. From the mentors' standpoint, making a contribution to the school and the student comes down to what Cole calls "enlightened self-interest. It cuts both ways. Students will be better prepared to succeed and industry will fill a critical need for talent."
4. *Accountability.* Each student takes the Society of Manufacturing Engineers exam at the end of the fourth year.
5. *Concentrations.* The program offers concentrations in parts manufacturing, product assembly, or factory management. In the third and fourth years there is considerable flexibility to choose electives and pursue special projects and coop assignments in the area of concentration.

WORK FORCE LITERACY—WHO CARES?

> Being able to read is so fantastic! It's the best high I've ever had. It's just a new beginning is what it is. It's like being reborn.
> *Bob Drogmund, Chip Scow Scheduler,*
> *Fir and Hemlock Division,*
> *Simpson Timber Co.*

For some companies, training and development starts with basic adult literacy. People need to master basic reading and writing skills before they can take a seat in a quality control training class.

Adult literacy is a shadow problem in the United States. Thousands of very bright motivated employees have managed to bluff, hide, and fake their way through school into the workplace. They need our help. Some who have been diagnosed as dyslexic may need even more help.

Companies like Simpson Timber have tried new approaches to this skill problem with an effort run mostly by employee volunteers for employees. Although tutors need to learn from a reading consultant how to recognize the three basic forms of reading problems, once they have done so, they can develop a learning program for each student.

CONCLUSION

There are many other individual examples of innovative workforce development programs like the ones from Motorola, Honda, and Wentworth Institute. Each initiative grew from the recognition that our work force will be around long after we have discarded that newest piece of high-tech capital equipment. For our manufacturing base to restructure and grow strong linkages forming "islands of excellence," all partners need to be equally skilled in the basics, Total Quality and JIT, as well as the other elements of Breakthrough Partnering: excellent communications, flexibility, an attitude of continuous improvement, a habit of collaboration, and trust.

Government and academia won't solve this problem. The answers must come from industry, often driven by big customers, the people who are closest to defining manufacturing needs, and the ones who have the most experience in developing solutions. The solutions won't be obvious until more industry leaders get moving and, like Dick Cole, start programs to develop the work force that industry needs for the next century.

FURTHER READING

For more on the Simpson Timber Adult Literacy Program, see
Dr. Dee Tadlock, Barbara W. Hinck, and Sandra Miller,
"Growing a Literate Workforce, Simpson Reads Right,"
Target, May–June, 1992, pp. 7–14.

CHAPTER 8

Enterprise Leadership

Once upon a time some water creatures lived under a bridge where they clung to the rocks and were safe. During the day the bridge sheltered them from the sun, and the Great River's current brought them tender morsels of edibles: They were comfortable. The river and the bridge gave them all they needed.

But there was one water creature who wanted to go downstream. What was out there? Would there be no food? Would ugly creatures devour him? He knew that if he left the little bridge, he would never get back upstream.

He discussed the big move with his neighbors, who all advised him to stay put. "It's different down there . . ."; "There are big hungry fish . . ."; "You won't make it, you'll be smashed on the rocks and die!"

But the quietness of the little bridge was not enough. So he set out. Saying goodbye to the others, he let go of his rock and drifted out into the river.

The current *did* take him and smash him against a rock. But instead of dying, the water creature floated downstream where the current was peaceful and serene, as he had never imagined it. And as he passed the other river creatures, they called out, "Look, a savior, a messiah!"

To which the little water creature replied, "No, all you have to do is let go."

Chris LaBonte, G & F Production Manager

*P*artnering leaders are unique. They must possess the usual business skills, plus an ability to assemble "the big picture" and to project their company's future into it. The challenge of leading partnership efforts is threefold. The leader must:

- Guide the organization to internal excellence
- Be an effective change driver
- "Team" with other professionals

INTERNAL EXCELLENCE

Partners must not set higher standards for colleagues than for themselves. First, leaders must move their organizations to excellence in areas critical to partnering: quality, timeliness, communications, flexibility, continuous improvement, the habit of collaboration, and trust. Building and leading internal excellence is an essential aspect of the drive for continuous improvement.

Dave Nelson of Honda describes how he learned to encourage continuous improvement amid the risks of trying new ideas. "Our associates see in daily management practices that we 'walk the talk,' we are sincere and our actions show what we believe. Deep loyalties are created as people realize that Honda's interest and theirs is one and the same. Associates come to believe that this is *their* business; they manage as if it's theirs." (All employees own at least one share of Honda stock.)

Nelson cites a number of unique philosophies responsible for the company's success. One is to "go to the spot," directly to the person who needs to know. "We don't hesitate to go to the president—it's not considered going around your boss." Honda demands making "high-risk" decisions. Nelson's advice to associates is, "Don't be afraid to step out in the deep water. When you do make a mistake, you have responsibility to tell your coworkers. No associate should have to bear the burden of a mistake himself."

There's a good reason for allowing mistakes at Honda. At his first board meeting, Nelson learned that the HAM president at that time, Mr. Yoshino, had bad news to report to the eight board members: Profitability had fallen short of previous projections. After Mr. Yoshino gave his report, nobody raised his or her voice, or threw shoes. Nelson was surprised. This was not like an American board meeting. Having expected the directors to be "looking for blood," he asked Mr. Yoshino why the reaction was so calm. "You must understand so that you use this [approach] in your management style. *What do you think would happen next time if the employee was pounced on when admitting to an error?* Next time he would shade the truth a little, or misrepresent the facts. We have to have the facts; nobody should ever be afraid to come to you."

How unlike the street-fighting most production and material people learn in the first days on the job. Managers shoot the bearer of bad news, so the lesson is: If you can't fix the problem, hide it!

CHANGE DRIVER

Many organizations that have racked up a series of internal team successes are surprised when their first partnering efforts fail. The problem may be their organizational structures, or an individual manager's style. A change driver must know how to get the organization to move to teaming. Leading an organization into and through major change involving new partnering relationships requires skills very different from those of a company working on other continuous improvement tasks.

Managers who were raised in a traditional hierarchy may not possess the current necessary team skills. Autocratic hierarchies leave little room for experimentation; they tend to reserve specific niches for specific decisions. A military organization is a typical example of a working hierarchy where command and control reign. The strength of the leaders in these organizations is an ability to receive much information from lower levels, to be the single integrator, and to take responsibility for decisions. But when external crises call for immediate, individual response, hierarchies are too slow in responding.

A Study in Contrasting Leadership Styles

Compare the organization structures and leadership styles of two early competitors, Digital Equipment Corporation and its spinoff, Data General. Operating in the same market, minicomputers and mainframes, their management and leadership styles, even the information systems that supported management, were complete contrasts. Digital took what could be called the "high road," depending on matrix management, individual effort, and internal political power structures to get product out. Creativity and initiative were encouraged. Digital stockroom clerks occasionally decided which customers had shipping priority, and new employees were expected to take a month or two to figure out what their jobs were. In contrast, Data General, although not a fun place to work, had a clear, very autocratic, and completely hierarchical organization structure. The company was run like a tight ship all the way to the bottom line. Data General job functions were tightly siloed; within fifteen minutes of landing in a cubicle, a new hire had her marching orders.

The character and actions of leaders determine the character and environment of the company. The contrasts between the two competitors became clearer as their leaders took opposite directions in growing their organizations. Legend says that DG was created when a Digital engineer, Edson DeCastro, broke with the company headed by Ken Olsen over a new product design and moved thirty miles down the street to found Data General. Hurt feelings and hatred ran deep. Two years after the split Digital employees were still forbidden to speak the words "Data General" aloud. Digital stayed with its matrix management approach, nicknamed "mattress management" by those who felt it allowed a lot of flopping around, while DG followed a strict command-and-control hierarchy.

As the companies grew and competed in the same markets, the bad feelings continued. When employees moved from Digital to DG, their decision was taken as the ultimate betrayal. Traitors who "jumped ship" were signed out and walked to the door within fifteen minutes of the announcement of their defection. Only one of the hundreds who left was allowed back by Digital.

The contrasts continued in the ways DeCastro and Olsen staffed and led their companies. DeCastro's crew, self-described "SOBs of the computer industry," played by their own set of rules. Digital played hard too, but seeing themselves as "the nice guys," they followed Olsen's lead and treated people better.

DeCastro's group had more sophisticated systems in place to guide hierarchical decision-making, and planners and buyers "lived by the system." Because the company was so carefully managed to the bottom line, even during its 100 percent growth stage most decisions took a very long time to process up from lower levels. A single vice president of manufacturing personally made all decisions on production rates, production mixes, capacity allocations, even customer order priorities.

Within a few years of its founding, spinoff DG ran up against barriers of its own creation. Its strong hierarchy and centralized decision-making faltered when the industry environment shifted from core to semiconductor memories.

First-generation computer memories, the kind that powered ENIAC and Whirlwind, consisted of thousands of vacuum tubes. Second-generation core memories consisted of strings of magnetized "donuts," many of which were produced by hand in Hong Kong. Like most other early computer technologies, they were expensive and slow and took time to produce. The third-generation semiconductor chips, although smaller and faster, came from an entirely different technology. In fact, at the time that semiconductor-based system's memory was first sold by DG, DG's very elaborate and all-encompassing MRP planning system called for 100 percent core memory and none of the new. Even though chip producers, still struggling with quality and design technology issues, were booked to capacity years in advance, even though failure rates were unpredictably high on first shipments, "the system" at DG called for no new memory components, and so none were ordered. By the time the production planner and the memory buyer had worked out their own differences on the exact appropriate mix and funneled their recommendations up the hierarchy, two precious months had passed. The resulting loss of market advantage was inevitable as competitors ate up limited semiconductor production capacity. The rigid, numbers-driven hierarchy had served the start-up well, but when big business shifts came down the turnpike, the DG vehicle took months to get out of the parking lot.

Strong partnering leaders need to be change drivers, to lead their companies into new territories. When they are not, as was the case of the leaders who missed the memory market, they take second place to the organization chart and become paper tigers.

TEAM LEADERSHIP

> Most work teams initially fail because purpose, objectives, and structure are not clearly defined and because unrealistic expectations of empowerment are created.
> *Donna Neusch, Partner, Millenium Management Tools*

The vice president of operations of a Midwest engine producer admitted to having difficulties with teams. "It just doesn't work. I wish somebody would tell us how to do it." The third and the newest challenge to management is that a leader must understand how to work in teams, and how to lead them. Although the phrase "leading a team" sounds like a contradiction in terms, American companies need to recognize that their partnerships will still require high-level, visible leadership.

The agreement between Boeing and its customer United demonstrates their high-level commitment to partnering. The partners worked for three weeks on a formal statement of their partnership, a summary of the team's objectives. The handwritten document was signed by executives from the customer and supplier team, including Philip Condit, Boeing's new president, and James M. Guyette, United's executive vice president of operations.

Leadership in partnering goes beyond signing up to work together on a specific project; it means setting in place the small details, the conditions that will allow other participants to work together. Team participants need to write down the details of their proposed relationship, to specify the types of meetings that will be set up to deal with certain types of issues, the location of the meetings, and the other partners to include, and when. Management's role is to monitor the process, not just the technical design in the case of Boeing, but the people process as well.

Leadership in teams doesn't always come from executive levels. At Williams Technologies, a South Carolina engine and transmission remanufacturer, the manager of quality assurance chaired a task force that created a new Williams Technologies–General Motors Powertrain rating system. Every month Williams's GM Powertrain customers visit Williams's South Carolina facility for a detailed quality review that rates Williams's supplier performance on a dozen criteria. (See Resource 3a.) In the spring of 1992 the customer suggested that Williams rate *them* as a customer. From this welcome suggestion a team of five managers developed the customer evaluation matrix. (See Resource 3b.)

Enterprise leaders also lead by example, by participating in the same partnering activities as their employees. John Krehbiel, Jr., president of Molex, the connector manufacturer in Lisle, Illinois, makes it a practice to participate in new company initiatives. When the company joined a customer-supplier consortium called NMX (NCR/Motorola/Xerox) to search for a common supplier quality review standard, Krehbiel himself completed two sections of the final evaluation instrument, the Motorola Quality System Review (QSR). For suppliers experienced in data gathering, completing the QSR can take one or two weeks, but areas of potential improvement may be recognized even sooner. Krehbiel spent only three days with NMX before realizing Molex's quality level could be improved.

His leadership and participation were crucial to the continued effort. At first, the idea of a QSR at Molex was far from popular. Some quality managers and process engineers, whose support was key to the program's success, were unsupportive. However, once the president decided that the audit would be worthwhile and signed on as a "data digger," the managers rallied and agreed to be a beta site for the consortium.

Slogging through the details eventually forced the company to boost its quality goals. "The QSR is among the most rigorous [audits] we have participated in. Initially, it hurt our feelings," Krehbiel says, but as a result, Molex committed to improving quality tenfold in the next three years.

Leadership Communications

Communicating direction is not always as easy as following specific rules in a policy manual. Sometimes a leader will make situations and choices clear nonverbally, like Dave King's color-coded parts trailer spearheading "localization" at Honda of America.

Leaders who guide their organizations into strong partnerships nurture skills on several levels. They understand both the technical as well as the people challenges—every day is a challenge. While they admit to not having all the answers, evidence of their ability to let team members innovate and find answers abounds. They know how to learn new behavior patterns frequently characterized by holding back, doing nothing when the urge is to fix it.

According to Alan F. Siebenaler, coauthor with Donna Neusch of *The High Performance Enterprise*, there are eight critical factors for team success:

1. A genuine shared case for change
2. An integrated, principle-based philosophy
3. The use of "hard" technologies—Kaizen, SPC (statistical process control), and other quality tools, and practical team training
4. A network of linkages back to the business objectives of the company
5. Definition: direction, operating boundaries, and other guidelines within which the teams will operate
6. Reinforcement
7. A viable implementation plan
8. An attitude of continuous improvement

Partnership leaders have high impact on Success Factors 1, 4, and 5. When management has identified the drivers of change and created a vision of the new partnership, they provide the organization with a shared understanding of direction. Partnering leaders, like Boeing's Condit and his United counterpart, have the responsibility to tie the new objectives back into the company's competitive goals. And finally, leaders must create the supportive organization structure on which partnering efforts proceed. They must also define the boundaries and specific tasks of the partnering teams.

When the president of a Southwest components producer decided to partner with a customer on a new product introduction, his first edict was "We will do a partnership team." It was followed by a flat response, then a flurry of meetings that stretched over days and weeks. So the product of his partnering edict was not the reduction in development time that he wanted. The team never operated with the right participants, or an appropriate list of objectives that would have harnessed his managers' enthusiasm. Employees came away with a general feeling of frustration: "We tried partnering, but it doesn't work."

Developing internal work teams is difficult enough. Extending partnering efforts to cover customer or supplier team members is clearly a greater challenge. Many traditional purchasing organizations and their skilled buyers and planners will not be active supporters of this exciting approach. The new leaders in partnering frequently come into supply management from other disciplines, with a full set of experiences satisfying diverse operating requirements, from operations management to engineering and quality assurance. Leaders will quickly recognize those who cannot make the journey, and after evaluation of the possibility of conversion to the philosophy of partnering, move quickly to select the best team members.

LEADERSHIP FOR DIFFERENT CORPORATE LIFE CYCLES

Just as not all current purchasing professionals are comfortable with partnering, not all managers will be the right ones to lead organizations into new partnering linkages. Look at the Three Wise Men.

The Three Wise Men: A Leadership Experiment

By 1975, a growing electronics assembler, National Electronics, had run out of inside talent for three inventory management positions to develop three different product segments: original equipment manufacturing (OEM), business products (commercial end users), and high-volume small systems (all users). The company had never recruited professional managers, and National's start-up successes had reinforced in-grown management styles. They were, however, obliged to go outside this time, and, as expected in some quarters, the three newcomers were greeted with mixed reactions and resistance.

Three very different managers were chosen and assigned to the three product lines. None of the newcomers knew in advance which business segment he or she would lead, and of course they didn't know which position they were interviewing for.

Position number one, OEM, was filled by a recent MBA with experience in mature large production operations. A "people person," Sal Ricardo prided himself on his personal skills and his ability to bring divergent, often competing groups together. His leadership style was more consensus and negotiation than driving; his finance skills guaranteed good accounting for the numbers. He was expected to be popular and a good fit.

Business products, the second largest but fastest-growing business segment, was headed by Jim Wallace, a grizzled, six-foot-two shipyard veteran, a heavy drinker and desk pounder. His background included no college degrees, since he had drunk himself out of MIT. Although his management style tended to hammer rather than lead employees, he could be counted on to deliver the goods, even if bloodied. Jim knew his intellectual limits, and depended on a few individuals for detailed business planning and financial projections.

The last position, high-volume small business, was taken by John Hunter, a tough ex–Navy Seal whose résumé included finance positions with several Fortune 500 companies. His first public offering, an elegant and at first glance achievable growth plan, was a hit. People skills and consensus were relatively unimportant to him; he expected to succeed by executing an elegant set of numbers. Those who "couldn't cut it were gone."

The first of the three to go was John Hunter. In National Electronics' people-oriented, no layoff environment, his rough treatment of employees was unacceptable. No parties, no end-of-quarter celebrations for him. Training and development dollars were targeted only for his hand-picked staff's use, to address very specific upcoming needs.

Second to go was Sal Ricardo. In his high-volume, high-pressure business there was little room for popularity and staff growth; daily ship targets took precedence. His political manoeuverings, often interpreted as vacillation and straddling the issue, undermined staff support. The last straw came when he missed two month's ship targets and failed to come down hard on the guilty parties.

The surviving Jim Wallace had a good run. For ten years his raucous results-at-all-costs leadership style satisfied growth objectives, winning him a few important supporters and many enemies. As long as his successes satisfied company needs and he kept moving, his feet never touched the detritus washed up by his wake. But when the company started its second generation, a slowed growth tempered by the appearance of real competitors, his own lack of professional skills and disinterest in the finer points of planning and control systems slowly reduced his effectiveness. The stress of working beyond his own abilities and heavy drinking took its toll. Within fifteen years his body broke down; he died suddenly, only three levels, but generations, away from the top.

The experiment had run its course, but what a damaging and wasteful way for a Fortune 500 organization to hire and develop managers. Selecting three very different types of managers to head up growing business segments was more than a calculated risk. It became a reflection of executive uncertainty. Leadership may be more an art than a science, but surely we know the difference between picking leaders for growth, or for plateaux, or turnarounds, or partnering. National couldn't decide, each of the three "management experiments" might have been appropriate for the company at a different stage in its life cycle.

Leadership for partnering has unique requirements. Of the three characteristics that describe partnering leaders—the ability to take their own organizations to excellence, to drive change, and the ability to work in and through partnership teams—the third characteristic is the most challenging. The key to building strong work teams, internal and external, is excellent communications and trust building. While managers aren't born with these skills, they and their partners can improve with practice. The leader's role in partnering initiatives, like the Boeing 777 customer-supplier team and the Williams Technologies–GM team, is to lay the groundwork and develop the rules and communications links and habits that will let the partnership grow. By actively participating in collaborations, like John Krehbiel and NMX, management can clearly mark the path and lead the way.

To move an organization into new areas, the successful leader must

1. Set an example
2. Make the partnership visible
3. Recognize and reward movement and successes
4. Not waste too much time on moving mountains and let the team make the journey
5. Expect that some people will not go on the journey; identify them, pick the new team players quickly, and keep moving

CHAPTER 9

Partnering Quality Basics

*M*adame Roz had a number for every occasion, and I needed a few to fill in the blanks. I was trying to understand the activity pattern, if there was one, in the thousands of orders, large and small, that entered General Lighting's vast distribution network. The problem was that if an unusually large customer request could not be filled by a particular distribution center, that order would be shunted to the side where an eighty-year-old warehouse veteran, Gilda, daily reviewed backlogged orders.

Here was a big, newly installed distribution requirements planning software package that ran well when orders fell within stocking levels. But large customer orders ("hits") crippled the system and caused great flurries of corporate-level expediting to ship the customer order and refill the pipeline.

A data processing screen to catch, or filter out, the large orders—replacing Gilda—seemed to be the answer. The screen would show a number calculated from the usage history. The idea was to review all the detail data, looking for activity patterns; the filter would be set at the high quantity that sent the system into the expedite mode. It was my expectation that such big hits were statistically "outliers on the standard distribution curve," or unusually large and infrequent orders. In fact when we calculated the standard deviation of the order size of a few products, we would be able to calculate a large order screen, set it at two or three standard deviations (sigma), and capture only those orders that hit the screen.

We had a definite problem with our approach. No single system carried an accurate detailed history of customer requests for specific quantities to ship on specific dates. All usage history was in fact history of what the fractured order fulfillment system eventually shipped to the customer, whether or not the shipment met the original request.

There was only one depository of data on customer requests—the Dragon Lady. Madame Roz's lair was lined floor to ceiling with green accounting folders. Her role, to protect and defend all relevant numbers at General Lighting, was described in corporate organization charts as "statistician" (and tennis partner to the president).

My first request, Did she have usage history on these products? met with a glacial response. Her red-laquered index finger pointed to the shelves. She had the numbers, all right. But the real question, rephrased after my sudden exit, became, Would she give me usage history on these products?

Sometimes analysis projects take radical turns. This temporary obstacle required high-level attention, or I would be using the return ticket to Boston earlier than we had planned. A behind-the-screen compromise was worked out. I would prepare six specific requests— on paper—and she would supply the appropriate answers—and not one number more.

The data transfer day appeared. With some excitement I waited. At promptly 8 A.M. Madame Roz appeared at her door—her two-inch red stillettos could carry her no farther—with a treasure chest of data, all mine.

The project proceeded on schedule. As hoped, a pattern emerged from entering a sampling of order hits. The screen was set at two sigma, or two standard deviations of activity. From that time forward, General Lighting order administration clerks could rely on the system to automatically capture and highlight oversized orders. And Madame Roz still had a number for every occasion.

In the mountain of accounting reports—from orders received to purchase orders, shipments, and invoices—Madame Roz had created a memorial to herself. Her Temple of Numbers had crippled the organization. There were too many to use. One simple request for usage history would take an input clerk six months to key in. Although the Dragon Lady had a number for every occasion, there was no linkage beyond the audit trail she protected so well. And all the data was well removed from its origins.

Five years before this encounter, Romey Everdell, who learned statistical analysis and problem-solving from Dorian Shainin, a Shewhart Quality Award winner, passed on his secret for making sense out of reams of meaningless and untranslatable numbers: "Let the data lead you." That simple statement is key to what customers and suppliers need to hear as they develop quality measurement and continuous improvement systems. Too much data is a distraction and a waste of resources.

All partners need to be skilled in the basics first. Advanced statistical techniques are appropriate where they are tied to specific enterprise objectives. If, say, learning QFD cannot be justified by the top corporate or quality officer, then QFD should be delayed until its application, if not the mechanics, is quite clear.

American companies have the ability to capture, analyse, and print more data than our organizations can effectively use. Unless you are a quality guru, your needs are simple. Customers need to know that the quality of product and service purchased from a supplier will match the product and process quality of your organization, so that the final customer shipment will be of highest quality. As a supplier, you need to understand your customer's quality specifications. You probably also want to know that the specifications are not beyond market requirements, and that the customer's quality measurement systems are consistent and meaningful.

Many companies analyze too much data, more than they can

digest, and certainly more than they need to attack basic communications and performance problems. How much better off General Lighting would have been with a few simple, well-understood, and well-thumbed activity reports, readable in the form of numbers, summaries, and visual data plots. In the hands of the users—in General's case, Gilda—a few trend and exception reports would have emptied out Madame Roz's office.

There is great precedent for data simplification. Mathematicians who developed the first atomic bomb did it with few mechanical aids beyond slide rules and rules of approximation. Not computer-dependent, they were operating in the world of art and science, where years of living with computations had allowed them to develop skills of approximation now lost since the advent of computer and calculator dependency. Before beginning computations they knew roughly how the final answer should look. That special skill allowed them to accelerate the Manhattan Project completion date to end World War II.

Raw numbers do not constitute usable data without good judgment. Customers don't want the responsibility of constant monitoring of supplier parts quality. The process must be controlled so that expected quality levels need not be continuously audited. Today, most supplier personnel have the quality systems in place to spot problems before they hit the receiving dock or point-of-use. Further, suppliers and customers must be able to communicate well the basic quality stats: process control, yield rates, trends, cost of quality, and specific problem areas.

The myth that more data from even more organizational functions will improve quality is commercially attractive to various quality consulting organizations and seminar houses. But myths, as we know, are exaggerations of a few simple human activities. Along with the trend to capture more data than can be used, we are seeing an extension of the purview of the quality gurus, a development that dilutes the quality focus.

Figure 9.1: The Quality Pyramid

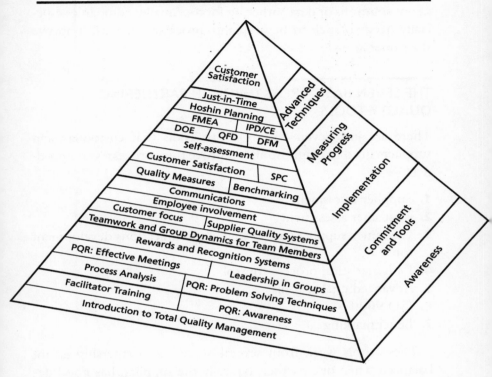

Too many "isms" and techniques built this giant, inflexible Quality Pyramid.

At the very bottom of the quality pyramid are the quality basics. As the pyramid rises higher and higher, each brick adds a new function to the total quality structure. Every pocket of the enterprise is included—from benchmarking and supplier quality systems to human behavior (human resources). The obvious question is: Where does this stop? The next one: Isn't the power of simple quality tools diluted as it encompasses each new function?

Very few organizations can afford to waste resources on extraneous solutions or data gathering forays. Smaller companies especially need to stick to basic quality processes that will improve their operations.

THE SEVEN BASIC BREAKTHROUGH PARTNERING QUALITY TOOLS

There are just Seven Basic Quality Tools that customers and suppliers need to diagnose and improve their processes and products:

1. Supplier assessment
2. Customer assessment
3. Customer-supplier partnership communications development tools
4. Basic statistical process control
5. Advanced quality tools
6. ISO 9000
7. Benchmarking

These tools work from several angles. A partnership is not balanced when one partner, typically the supplier, has good detailed data on product quality performance, but none describing how that product performs downstream, in the hands of the customer.

Communications account for 90 percent of the success of customer-supplier partnerships. Tools 1 through 5 are intended in particular to give partners necessary information to improve their partnership. The better communications instruments are written so that they become continuous improvement aids, not another hammer that can be turned on suppliers. No. 1, supplier assessment, which can be performed by the customer or by the supplier company itself, reviews supplier product and process quality. No. 2, customer assessment, looking from the other side of the fence, allows suppliers to look at potential customers and evaluate how their policies and attitudes will work in a partnership arrangement. No. 3, customer-supplier communications development tools, encompasses questions of trust and meeting financial terms.

No. 4, basic statistical process control, is the short list of basic quantitative tools that measure and highlight process control problems. This group represents the "Quality 101" tools that everyone in an enterprise must use well. No. 5, advanced quality tools, like QFD and various Japanese imports (Poke-yoke, Hoshin planning), while they may not be requirements for basic supply management operations, are used by many world-class organizations. At a minimum, the world-class supply management organization will be familiar with, if not using, these advanced tools.

Let's look at each of the Seven Breakthrough Partnering Quality Tools in more detail.

1. SUPPLIER ASSESSMENT

There are numerous customized supplier development protocols, among them Chrysler's Pentastar, GM's PICOS (Purchase Input Concept Optimization with Suppliers), HAM's BP (Best Position, Best Productivity, Best Product, Best Price, Best Partners) Program, Ford's Q1, McNeil's Valued Partners, NCR's Supplier Development Process, and the Motorola Quality System Review (the QSR). All of these and other less well known programs rate and categorize supplier performance. Superior suppliers earn various forms of recognition, in addition to by-passing customer inspections and shipping directly to point-of-use. NCR's Supplier Development Process classifies suppliers into six performance categories:

S1 Certified—The highest level of preference for a supplier commodity.

> *S2 Committed*—The supplier and NCR are jointly committed to working toward a level of relationship and performance necessary to be considered an S1 supplier.

> *S3 Targeted*—The supplier has been singled out by NCR for development to S1 status.

> *S4 Preferred*—NCR prefers to do business with the supplier for a given commodity since the risk is considered to be minimal.

> *S5 Tactical*—NCR does business with the supplier only where a tactical need exists, even though no decision has been made to enter into a partnership with the supplier for a given commodity.

> *S6 Phaseout.*

All supplier assessment programs begin with basic measurement of supplier process, product, and performance records. Some, like the Motorola QSR, progress beyond measurement to diagnose and help solve problems. Fundamental to supplier certification is performance measurement and ongoing monitoring. A very simple supplier certification should include questions about existing quality programs, results, housekeeping, age and maintenance of capital equipment, record-keeping, payment terms, and quality organization issues.

Motorola Quality System Review (QSR)[1]

The Motorola QSR is a comprehensive model for supplier performance review. This assessment instrument preceded the Baldrige Award by a few years. In fact, by the time the national award was created, Motorola was already familiar with the quality review process. The document is written so that assessment scores can easily be turned into improvement opportunities. As a result, its Maturity Index becomes a very useful project planning tool, what Ken Stork, former Motorola director of purchasing and materials, describes as "a take-home exam with Cliff Notes."

The QSR contains ten sections ("subsystems"), each of which breaks down into a series of questions asked by the reviewer, followed by a list of "considerations" characterizing elements of performance on this particular question.

MOTOROLA QSR SUBSECTIONS

1. Quality system management
2. New product/technology/service development control
3. Supplier (internal or external) control
4. Process operation and control
5. Quality data programs
6. Problem-solving techniques
7. Control of quality measurement equipment and systems
8. Human resources involvement
9. Customer satisfaction assessment
10. Software quality assurance

The third part of each question includes descriptive scoring ranging from Poor to Outstanding. For example, Section 1, Quality System Management, contains eleven questions that review the quality functions and policies in place. The excerpt below focuses on the first question in Subsystem 1.

EXCERPT OF THE MOTOROLA QSR, SUBSYSTEM 1

1.1 Is there a quality function or well-defined organization that provides customer advocate guidance to the total organization, and is this position fully supported by management?

Considerations
a. The organization's quality management reports at the appropriate level within the organization to assure an effective quality system.
b. The quality function performs final product acceptance audits and tracks internal defects as well as field hardware and software defects.

c. The organization has a documented new product release procedure with appropriate signature authority to stop the release if the product/service is not deemed ready for release.

d. A clear method exists for customers to communicate quickly with this group about quality issues.

Scoring

Poor: There is no quality function or organization.

Weak: The beginnings of a system exist.

Fair: A quality function exists, is defined, and is working in some areas.

Marginally qualified: The quality function is active in most but not all areas.

Qualified: Quality function is well defined and supported; audit results are acted upon quickly.

Outstanding: Role of quality function recognized and supported at all levels; it guides the organization and has strategic impact.

Subsystem 3 of the QSR focuses on supplier (internal or external) control. This section includes a series of questions, followed by considerations containing more detailed descriptions of how these questions might be answered. All questions in this section lead companies to complete the first step in world-class partnering: supplier assessment and certification, in a positive and constructive way, by phrasing questions that encourage the world-class customer to provide information to help the supplier improve.

EXCERPT OF MOTOROLA QSR, SUBSYSTEM 3

1. Are requirements defined, communicated, and updated to ensure that the supplier understands expectations?

2. Does a system exist that measures the performance of the supplier and communicates such information to the suppliers?

3. Have the organization's processes been characterized to identify the critical requirements for the supplier's products?

4. Have the capabilities of the supplier's process been assessed and considered in the establishment of the requirements?
5. To what extent have partnerships been established with suppliers and assistance provided to ensure that each supplier has the capability to consistently supply conforming product?
6. Have quality and cycle time metrics improvement goals been established participatively with the supplier?
7. Has a system been established with the supplier for identification and verification of corrective action?
8. Have the requirements for supplied materials been properly characterized and specified to ensure conformance of the product/service to customer satisfaction requirements?
9. Is there an effective supplier certification program or equivalent supplier continuous quality-improvement program?
10. Can all personnel who contact suppliers properly reflect appropriate quality-improvement programs and status to them?

Each question is scored poor to outstanding on a "maturity index." Performance in a specific function is evaluated in three categories of application—approach, deployment, and results. An organization might, for example, have a good approach to tracking shipments, with procedures in place for fixing problems but with no documentation of measurable results. If procedures written in a manual are not clear and are not well understood by administrators, the scoring will reveal the discrepancy between documentation and actual problem-solving ability.

The Baldrige Award

When a company decides to go for the Malcolm Baldrige National Quality Award, there is a tremendous impact on the activities of everyone in the organization, including supply management. Participants agree that the audit process is grueling, but everyone—particularly those who don't win—learns from it. Companies that have applied for the Baldrige have already assembled the quality information that partnerships require, and the application process itself supports continuous improvement.

But competing for a Baldrige can be humbling. Bill Jastrow, director of materials at Amdahl Corporation of Sunnyvale, California, says that before applying for the national award, his company had completed its own internal performance evaluation. Amdahl considered itself "world-class in many areas. We thought we had a good chance of winning." But in the final rounds, Amdahl failed. What happened?

When the Amdahl team started preparations for the Baldrige site visit, they asked companies who had been through the experience what to expect. The team learned that the examiners look for proof of sustained performance improvement.

For Amdahl, lack of documentation proved to be a fatal weakness. The Baldrige examiners considered statements about supplier visits without documented trip reports anecdotal. Although Amdahl had started quality-improvement programs in 1983, its strongest advances were in the late eighties. But trip reports were saved for only one year. Luckily, one manager had saved minutes of quality-improvement meetings dating back to 1983, which offered examiners some proof of the company's efforts—agendas, names of meeting leaders, and other supporting details that verified these improvement activities.

As a result of the Baldrige process, the company does a much better job of record-keeping. Now, when a buyer helps a supplier resolve a technical or quality issue, the buyer lets engineering know and a written record is kept.

Amdahl's weakest area was benchmarking, Breakthrough Partnering Quality Tool 7, which is also covered in the QSR. Examiners commented that Amdahl needed to do more comparisons, and that the goals for benchmarking should have been higher. This defect turned into a continuous improvement opportunity when the company became one of the participating companies in the Center for Advanced Purchasing Studies (CAPS) benchmarking survey. More Amdahl employees became regulars at local NAPM meetings, and the company sponsored a Bay Area benchmarking study.

One company that did win the award is California-based contract manufacturer Solectron Corporation, an example of the adage "Practice makes perfect." Despite winning forty-one various quality and service awards from customers, it took two unsuccessful Baldrige applications before the 1991 win. For Solectron, working up to the award was key to their continuous improvement process. The Baldrige examiners noted weak internal communications and community involvement. The feedback from these audits provided a springboard from which Solectron developed a work plan. The company started Solectron University, did a customer/executive survey to determine how the customer felt about the firm, and set up a benchmarking program. "When we found out we had won, there was delirium," said Tom Allison, vice president of materials at the Milpitas facility.

One of Solectron's innovative approaches to improving internal communications and building to Six Sigma quality is a morning meeting series developed by chief executive Winston Chen. Chen believes the company should "let everybody learn to be a general manager." Tuesday's meeting is dedicated to training. The meeting on Wednesday covers quality issues and feedback from production. Thursday is customer feedback day.

There are other benefits to a Baldrige application. The site visit was a big reward for Solectron. The company established "defense teams" to prepare for the audit. When the examiners arrived for their four-day visit, 700 out of 2,600 employees—many more employees than usual—got to talk with the experts.

Even after winning the award, Solectron still has some areas—like supplier partnering and information management—that need improvement, according to Allison. For example, in 1991 the parts-per-million quality goal was 1,350; actual ppm was 3,000. With a much improved score in 1992, the goal was 233 against an actual of about 1,500.

For those organizations that have a chance of progressing to a a site visit (the last and most challenging phase of the audit) the value of a Baldrige application is generally accepted. But as one Chicago-area three-time applicant discovered, when you don't get a site visit on the third try, it's probably time to stop the hoopla and try something else that will be less disruptive and more basic.

The Baldrige has been criticized from the perspective that it is possible to win the award and lose the business. At least one 1990 winner, Wallace Company, has fallen on hard times. The document contains no mechanism to measure financial profitability or business viability.

As Amdahl's Bill Jastrow noted, application for the Baldrige Award is a useful continuous improvement exercise—even invaluable to their organizations. Most world-class organizations, in addition to making award applications, develop comprehensive quality-improvement programs like supplier development programs at Ford, Chrysler, Xerox, and Honda of America.

Honda of America's BP Program is a model of supplier measurement and development. The program goes beyond measurement of product quality, moving into suppliers' organizations to help them improve.

Forty-five Honda of America suppliers have signed up for the program, whose goals include "genshi 15 percent," which means cost reduction combined with other improvement factors, a two-fold productivity increase, reduction of defects, and self-reliance. The program takes on both a hard and soft focus. Soft BP, the initial focus, includes associate (Honda and the supplier) involvement, and other initiatives such as housekeeping, obtaining tools for operators, and other activities that build commitment and trust. Soft BP activities require minimal investment, but they typically yield better raw material utilization while reducing waste.

Soft BP paves the way for "hard BP" activities, tooling and other improvements that would require capital investment. Ninety percent of the customer-supplier development process at Honda is communications, and 10 percent is technical.

The Downside of Supplier Assessments

A full assessment and follow-up review, like the QSR, is not an exercise completed by one individual in an afternoon. Completing the document takes input from many different segments of an organization, and requires forty to eighty hours to complete. Because customers need suppliers who are expert at quality *processes*, not quality *audits*, customers need to focus their certification efforts so that they don't detract from the supplier's real mission.

Molex, the Lisle, Illinois, half-billion-dollar connector supplier to NCR, Motorola, and Xerox—has an interesting lesson to tell. In one year the Lincoln, Nebraska, plant was hit with twenty-one quality audits and certification exercises, totaling one man-month of time. Why couldn't a few of these customers agree on a single certification standard? Ray Stark, at that time head of Xerox purchasing, Ken Stork, formerly of Motorola, and Al Raepour of NCR met to brainstorm a solution. They exchanged and critiqued their own supplier certification programs; the QSR was the one rating system that all three Molex customers found most appropriate for their requirements.

The group met to map out a pilot run. Molex President John Krehbiel, Jr., completed two of the QSR sections himself. The customers were happy with Molex's QSR results and expect further quality improvements at other Molex plants.

2. CUSTOMER ASSESSMENT

In Somerville, South Carolina, Williams Technologies, a supplier of remanufactured engine components, was accustomed to monthly quality reviews by one of its major, and very demanding, customers, GM Powertrain. Williams's Performance Matrix (see Resource 3a) evaluated Williams's performance in twelve areas. Total scores became an important month-to-month figure that the entire organization focused on. Six months ago a GM customer representative suggested that Williams rate *them*. Williams people were very receptive to the opportunity to give structured feedback. Peggy Goddard, Williams's quality assurance manager, remarked, "They will have no doubt [about] what is important to us."

From this welcome suggestion, a Williams team developed the customer evaluation matrix. How did the supplier notify its primary customer that they were indeed going to start a report card? "Very delicately," answers Peggy.

How customer assessment questionnaires are used—protocol —is as important as their contents. At Williams, users on both sides of the table feel this is a perfect communication tool as well as providing a quantitative presentation of quality performance. The monthly product review meeting includes discussion of both the customer and the supplier rating schemes. One month in advance, Peggy faxes agenda topics to GM for input and agreement on how the meeting will be run. Twelve to fourteen participants attend, of which ten are from Williams, including managers from production manufacturing, quality, technology and productivity, materials, personnel, and occasionally marketing. The customer speaks first; Williams goes last.

Although GM rates its supplier in twelve categories of service performance, six of which fall under quality, not all criteria are weighted equally. In percentages, the customer's biggest concerns are warranty exposure (18), sediment (finished machining quality—14), and continuous improvement (14). The total score adds up to 100 percent. On the other hand, the Customer Evaluation Sheet (see Resource 3b) contains fewer rating elements, and is tailored to the small company's concerns: schedule, parts delivery, new parts quality, communications, price/cost, and customer-supplier relationship. The most heavily weighted factors are scheduling and price/cost. In June 1992, for example, GM's adherence to schedule was rated a high 9, multiplied by a weight of 15, to produce a total value for keeping to schedule of 135.

Fortunately for the participants, humor makes the pill a little easier to swallow. Williams's Points of Measure show detailed gradations of customer performance to schedule, from absolute perfection (multiple truckloads, no changes in a month, no mix changes in a week, no emergencies), down to "Thankful for the business!"

Customers react with varying degrees of tolerance to being rated. Fred Bejster, GM Powertrain Service Engineer, says, "Our customer-supplier relationships have always been a strong point with any of the remanufacturing suppliers we work with. We want to be very interactive with them, assuring good product quality and on-time shipments. We had a good relationship to begin with." Although the customer's rating sheet started partly as a joke, when supplier personnel ran with it, everybody in the plant got involved in developing the criteria. The original scores were low, "a real shock. Guess they didn't want to inflate our ego!" Since then, the exchange of ratings has helped improve communications and has given the GM representative some helpful feedback to take back to other functionally separated GM divisions. The expectation is that the customer evaluation document should help make other functions more responsive and responsible.

The best way for a customer to understand how well she or he is communicating with a supplier is, of course, to ask. But realistically, most big customers are not accustomed to giving frank and useful feedback to their suppliers. The responsibility for structuring that feedback via a dynamic communications and improvement tool like Williams's rests with suppliers, the partners who have much to gain from better customer behavior.

Rating of customers by suppliers is a new practice, one that has not entered the realm of standardization. The approach ranges from the friendly customer asking, "How are we doing?" which warrants eliciting an ambivalent supplier response of, "You're just fine, thank you!" to very detailed instruments that truly offer opportunities for mutual improvement.

3. CUSTOMER-SUPPLIER PARTNERSHIP DEVELOPMENT TOOLS

There are three customer-supplier partnership development tools: partnership agreements, protocol, and supplier councils. Communications and protocol are the most important elements in building trust and developing a partnership that extends beyond contractual legal agreements. Helene Fine, a researcher in customer-supplier partnering, describes a successful three-step partnering process:

1. Uncover mutual advantages.
2. Respect and rely on each other's technical expertise.
3. Know what motivates and drives your partner.[2]

Partnership Agreements

Different companies approach the partnership with various formal statements of their intent, ranging from contracts to formal but nonbinding partnership statements to handwritten one-page collaboration documents. The best collaborative agreements share the following characteristics:

- *They are written and signed by the people who will either make up the day-to-day working partnership or who, as top managers, will take a very visible and active role in the partnership.* The Boeing-United partnership document, signed by the executive officers of the customer and supplier, took three weeks to develop. In its final form the document was handwritten.

- *They are simple and define the intent of the partnership for all parties.* They do not, however, specifically define day-to-day operating practices. The one-page Boeing-United partnership agreement marks the beginning of a relationship that involved many purchasing and engineering personnel, but the team and their work are not mentioned in the document. The specifics could not be predicted at the time the agreement was created.

- *The agreement typically takes three to five weeks to complete.* The documents are simple and driven by mutual agreement, reducing the hundreds of partnership details—expected tasks and completion dates, the working paperwork, the team functions—to a single sheet of paper. The process of reaching consensus, which requires each party to cover most of the possibilities of greatest concern, takes time. Throughout the process of developing the agreement, the parties are working out the three-step process, setting limits, discovering mutual interests, and assigning responsibilities based on individual expertise.

Protocol

Protocol not only sets the stage for the kind of behavior we want to see in a partnership, but it is also a reflection of the importance of the partnering commitment. Hitler retaliated for Germany's humiliation after World War I by accepting France's World War II capitulation in the same railroad car that had been used the first time. He took an event of protocol as an opportunity to dramatically set the stage for Germany's occupation of France, and to make a worldwide statement of his ongoing intent.

Protocol prescribes the conduct of business, the creation of a formal meeting agenda and follow-up meeting evaluation check-lists, entry and exit rules, and the activities of a good facilitator. The checklist in Resource 6 helps participants monitor whether meetings are working well. Even the best projects can be dragged astray if they lack such instruments (see AME Meeting Evaluation, Resource 6).

When secondary agendas lie beneath the surface of ongoing working meetings, it should be not be a surprise when the group's results don't meet *stated* objectives. A consortium of government, consulting, and a few industry leaders illustrates this frequently encountered problem. Originally pitched as a coming together to fund small suppliers' training needs, the project fell apart as each constituency struggled to promote secondary agendas not stated in the protocol. The consultants, looking for big training con-tracts, tried to define the group's task as supplying commercially attractive, expensive doses of politically acceptable Total Quality training. The government people, not knowing their way around a factory floor, resisted specific input from manufacturing leaders, particularly suppliers, about their daily work force needs. And the academics, one foot in each camp, seeing a commercial and pro-motion opportunity, tailored their proposals to suit the available faculty resources. The final group product reflected the partici-pant interest groups' relative strength, which overwhelmed the small voice of the beleaguered small supplier.

Supplier Councils

Although supplier councils are not intended in themselves to be partnering activities, to organizations like the Foxboro Company, control systems manufacturer, and Honda, they are important opportunities to communicate and build trust. By opening lines of communication they build better business relationships. Cus-tomers can use the supplier meeting or supplier advisory council as an opportunity to keep suppliers informed of critical and changing issues like schedules, organization structures, and quality specifications.

Although the impetus for setting up supplier councils must come from top management, representatives to the meetings should come from working areas like engineering, procurement, and manufacturing. Operating personnel who are closest to the loci of measures that will improve cash flow or reduce cycle time must be involved.

Protocol is especially important when competing suppliers participate in advisory meetings. If the customer/host has not worked out protocol details well in advance, competing suppliers should not be invited to the same conference.

4. BASIC STATISTICAL PROCESS CONTROL (SPC)

Some people make SPC into a mysterious academic routine, but it needn't become a tool for the elite. There are a half dozen basic quality tools that will allow any team member or supply manager to measure, test, and monitor any process, from order entry to distribution systems to supplier quality and production processes.

There are three guidelines to building a basic statistics quality toolkit:

Guideline 1. Use and understand a few simple tools

Flow chart—The visual description of a process, including stops for various operations and wait times

Pareto analysis—The categorization of problems and analysis of the frequency with which they occur

Run chart or plot—Graphs that capture measurable characteristics as they occur

Histogram and scatter diagram—Tracks and plots that show the occurrence of specific problems with the object of discovering patterns or trends

Calculations: average, standard deviation, and Cpk (a measure of process capabilities)

Guideline 2. Be consistent

Decide which measurements are relevant at the beginning of an improvement process, and stick with them. Save the supporting data that is summarized or displayed in visual plots. You may change the output, but save the basic history, or chronological record, should you decide to try a different calculation or plot on the data. A word about history—save a minimum of three periods of data (three is the magic number that will show trends or cycles—two will not). Without a baseline and several sequential periods of good data, the exercise turns from improvement to meaningless data collection.

Guideline 3. Look for patterns

Whenever data can also be displayed visually, plot it first to look for patterns on a histogram or a scatter diagram. Do calculations only after the data form a meaningful pattern from which calculations will identify key problem factors.

5. ADVANCED QUALITY TOOLS

Supply managers use the basic quality tools in day-to-day interactions with upstream suppliers and downstream customers. Advanced quality tools such as QFD (Quality Function Deployment) and Kaizen, or Hoshin planning, while they are not part of ordinary problem-solving and data-gathering activities, are important for supply managers to understand. And larger suppliers and customers may be using these tools in new product development teams.

A typical QFD application might be the design of a new aircraft to include all customer service quick-turnaround benefits. The supplier's design team would use QFD to uncover and consider as many of these issues as possible early in the design effort. This exercise proves to be a very deliberate approach to design; typically, it is, however, not well understood or accepted by many functional areas in an organization, and its complexity tends to offer more than many groups need.

Hoshin planning, another advanced quality tool, is a comprehensive approach to large projects. A West Coast instrumentation producer is using Hoshin to develop a new management information system for the next decade. Each group in the planning process is focusing on the corporate objective: to develop a new system that will satisfy all cross-functional as well as individual needs. Within each functional group, planning and brainstorming activities are focused on that single goal.

6. ISO 9000

First used in the United States in the late 1980's, ISO 9000 was developed by the International Organization of Standardization in Geneva, in which the United States is represented by the American National Standards Institute.[3] Many questions surround ISO 9000: whether a company needs to be registered, which products are covered, who performs registrations and audits, and what registration means. The issue has resisted simplification, as the commercial interests of various quality groups and hordes of consultants and training houses capitalize on suppliers' fear of being locked out of major business segments. In spite of the conflicting viewpoints, ISO 9000 registration is a valuable quality tool for the purpose of both seeking to sell to European markets and satisfying customers who require evidence of a quality process.

ISO standards prescribe a process that builds consistency and repeatability. But the standards do not actually specify how a product should be built for highest quality or what the tolerance for defects should be. Indeed, in Europe ISO is described as a driver's license: It gives the bearer permission to drive, but it doesn't guarantee that he will stay on the road!

Instead, ISO concentrates on certifying that a company has procedures, including documentation, in place to support a quality assurance system. Next, the audit checks to see if the company is in compliance with its own procedures.

Preparing for an ISO assessment, like getting ready for any other certification, requires considerable time and money (some companies estimate spending $15,000 or more to get started). The average time to achieve registration is twelve to sixteen months, although EMC Corporation managed to complete the process in five months. The examination typically involves a two- to four-day site visit.

Is the process a useful one? The response is mixed. The president of a Connecticut electroplating firm feels that since his company already sells in Europe, pursuing ISO registration at this time would be a diversion of resources. Some organizations want to work on actual quality improvements, feeling that ISO addresses documentation issues more than process excellence. But to Carl Davis, ISO project leader at Duracell, Inc.'s, Worldwide Technology Center, the effort has been extremely rewarding. Duracell's ISO project team was aware that it had to document quality procedures. They created three levels of documentation intended to assess employee commitment: documentation control, design control, and instrument calibration.

According to Gary C. Cowles, director of corporate purchasing at Southwire Company in Carrolton, Georgia, ISO strengthens discipline as it demands formal procedure manuals that are also flexible enough to adapt to changing customer requirements. His expectation is that as his own company completes registration, his suppliers, like the suppliers to Baldrige-winning Motorola, will follow suit.

7. BENCHMARKING

The term *benchmarking* has bounced through various definitions to mean a variety of things to different users and consultants. Originally the term had a technical definition meaning to compare the capabilities of a system or process to some standard. The definition of benchmarking includes making comparisons between partners who want to improve their processes.

Nowadays, useful data on specific areas come from other companies, particularly those considered excellence models, like Motorola and Federal Express, and a few data bases, notably that of the American Productivity and Quality Center.

Unfortunately, the scope of benchmarking has expanded, like TQM, to a point of dilution. In the areas of customer-supplier partnering, supply management, purchasing, and material management, there are few easily accessed sources of comparison data. Practitioners of benchmarking in these areas need to nail down the specific points of comparison and target areas for improvement before locating a benchmarking partner. As Ken Stork advises, would-be benchmarking partners need to do their own homework before they call for help from other companies.

Benchmarking is important to both customer and supplier partners. The most important first step in any benchmarking project is to limit the number of data points that will be studied to ensure that the most valuable areas will be examined. A company needs to identify specific practices to focus improvement efforts on, and to set goals to aim for. For example, if your order administration fills up total cycle time, then benchmark against a partner, like a retailer, that has order perfected administration.

The rules for benchmarkers are simple:

1. Clarify your own performance before taking on the full project.
2. Be clear on your objectives.

"TAKE WHAT MATTERS MOST"

Hunched over an eight-inch-thick warehouse inventory printout, I was kept busy by Madame Roz's data as I entered row after row of numbers into my new programmable calculator. Each computation took several seconds to grind out, and it was hard to keep my mind in place as the numbers marched on. The exercise took on a familiar rhythm: punch, punch, punch, check, wait, read, scribble, punch, punch, punch, check . . . I remembered a similar scene fifteen years earlier. My first purchasing job required me to enter columns of handwritten service invoices on a two-ton Frieden calculator. At least the noise kept me awake. "You've come a long way, baby," I thought.

The fire alarm broke my reverie. Ruthie, the clerk with whom I shared an ancient black telephone, jumped. "It's a fire!" she screamed. "Follow me!"

"Follow me" meant to run, not walk, to the nearest and only exit from the building that we later nicknamed the Triangle Shirtwaist Factory. The fire escape, a wooden stairwell that ran down seven flights next to the freight elevator, past the paint shop and the box storage area, was filling up fast with people. We had to move—we could already hear the sirens.

"Take what matters most," Ruthie advised, as she secured her green lizard designer purse across her shoulder. I had a quick decision to make. What if someone stole the calculator that held days of input work? Or should I carry the eight-inch printout and all the supporting transaction sheets down seven flights? And I knew that if I left behind my precious Italian briefcase and bag they would be gone when, and if, we returned. What would you take?

A closing word on partnering quality tools:
Take what matters most.

NOTES

1. All passages in this chapter paraphrased and excerpted from the Motorola Corporate Quality System Review Guidelines, adopted by the Motorola Corporate Quality Council, March 1991, are used with the permission of Motorola, Inc.

2. Helene Fine, "The Manufacturer Supplier Interface: A Case Study of the Making of a Relationship," unpublished paper, Spring 1992.

3. A book spelling out ISO 9000 standards is available from American National Standards Institute, 11 West 42nd St., New York, NY 10036. See also Asbjorn Aune and Ashok Rao, "ISO 9000 Standards: A Baseline for Excellence, *Target*, September–October 1992, pp. 23–29.

CHAPTER 10

On Being a
World-Class Customer

The reality is that most companies are too busy doing "market research" to learn from their customers and too busy setting "quality standards" for suppliers to learn from them.

Michael Schrage, Los Angeles Times *industry analyst*

One of Motorola's best printed-circuit-board suppliers wanted to reduce his scrap and rework expense. The factory had to deal with too many inconsistencies of specifications, multiple quality requirements, and other special needs from a range of customers; all contributed to his costs and resulted in errors.

His conclusion? He had too many customers. He decided to "fire" five. This supplier needed customers who listened to his production and design issues, who respected schedule stability, customers who reinforced their stated willingness to partner with him in the long term with accessibility and commitment.

Motorola had offered world-class engineering and training help. The communications sector they supplied was a growing, white hot competitive market. Motorola and two other good customers were OK—and he had two openings available!

Being a good customer matters for a very obvious but typically overlooked reason: It takes two companies to make a partnership.

Making demands on suppliers without giving them the information they need to do a good job limits their performance. The first stage of supplier development, when suppliers improve their process capabilities and product quality to levels acceptable in the marketplace, is already an accepted, expected fact. To be a healthy player in the subcontracting electronics business, for example, suppliers must produce at the defect level of fewer than one hundred to two hundred parts per million. To be highest in quality and attract Baldrige-quality customers, defects must drop down to the single digits. The next challenge—very high levels of quality, reduced delivery time, and excellent service—requires assistance and cooperation from customers. Suppliers like Solectron need to know more about customer product applications so that they can, for example, select the best components for their design.

To be strong partners, companies must look at both sides of the fence. Supplier certification and development programs are not enough; purchasers must also be world-class customers.

FOUR CLEAR ADVANTAGES TO BEING A "BEST CUSTOMER"

1. Cost Savings

World-class customers lower their administrative costs by communicating more effectively with their suppliers. They remove administrative and management layers that interfere with communications and increase headcounts. Significant cost savings by EMC, Bose, Apple, Intel, and others have been achieved by locating supplier representatives on site. These "in-plants" work as sales representatives, master schedulers, and buyer-planners, as discussed in Chapter 3. Typically in-plants eliminate at least two layers from the supply chain, the salesman and the buyer-planner, thereby reducing overhead costs.

2. Time Savings

World-class customers cut lead times by giving suppliers as much information as they can early in the process. Supplier representatives sit on the product design team, as Boeing did in the development of the 777 twinjet.

Time accumulates in the most expensive phase of a product cycle, the design phase, when sourcing, design, and manufacturing process decisions add up to total cycle time. This is especially true with manufacturers who outsource big chunks of their product, like Sun Microsystems and other systems integration/software houses. The daily communications grind, combined with monthly customer-supplier meetings, chews up valuable market time.

PictureTel, a Massachusetts producer of teleconferencing systems, found a way to short-cut coast-to-coast airplane time with Solectron, their Silicon Valley board supplier. The East Coast customer has given its supplier a full teleconferencing system that, at a cost of approximately $15 to $20 per hour plus the initial $20,000 to $80,000 investment, beats the cost of shuttling purchasing people away from their offices for three or four days at a time. For Kevin Jean, PictureTel's purchasing manager, the regular Friday-at-two videoconferencing meetings are a joy. In addition to discussing schedule and quality issues, participants can transmit designs and other paperwork at the same time via the document camera.

3. Better Products and Processes

Michael Schrage, *Los Angeles Times* industry analyst and a researcher at MIT's Sloan School of Management, recounts a story from Procter & Gamble chief executive E. L. Artzt. The consumer products giant had a terrible problem with its Pampers disposable diapers. The company was having trouble mass-producing the thin rubber leggings that stop those critical leaks.

According to Artzt, the thinness of the rubber caused it to "creep" and made high-speed production of the diapers virtually impossible. This problem could cost the company millions.

In desperation, Procter & Gamble did something it had never done before: It invited the supplier into the plant to take a look. The supplier looked at the problem and said two words, "Golf balls." It turns out that the supplier was the leading manufacturer of the ultrathin, tightly wound rubber filaments that form golf ball cores, which gave the supplier the expertise to solve P & G's production problem with a minimum of fuss and expense.[1]

World-class customers improve their technology and process knowledge when they draw on specialized expertise that naturally resides within highly focused suppliers. They also share their training and development resources. EMC, a storage systems producer, depends on commodity suppliers of components like Seagate for design and process insights. The Seagate-EMC partnership was not always successful, however. Seagate became EMC's "premier (drive) vendor" only after competitor Hitachi threatened Seagate's business. Hitachi reliability as measured in mean time between failures had reached over one million hours, higher than Seagate's. Mike Schoonover, VP of operations at EMC, remembers "Black Friday," when he informed Seagate that their status as a supplier was endangered.

"Tactically, we had to fix [Seagate's] product because they had the product we wanted." He conducted a "cold gray light of dawn" meeting at the supplier's Minneapolis office. The talk was very direct and open, "the kind of conversations you would normally have with family—through thick and thin." All Seagate had to do was match Hitachi quality levels, and the long-term partnership with EMC was theirs.

Seagate signed up for the partnership program by putting a senior vice president in charge of making a cultural change. The customer conducted aggressive process audits, pointed out problems, and made recommendations to make significant changes in test protocols. EMC also performed extensive employee training at Seagate using some continuous improvement and reliability modeling. "We are experts at disk drive quality, so we made all our corporate resources available."

The supplier commitment to develop the "million-hour drive" was not an evolutionary migration; improvements would appear on current products, with quantum improvements on future designs. "Reliability is design, design, design" was the charge.

For a company that wants to focus on high-quality, well-marketed mass storage systems, it makes sense to leave the design and production of critical technologies to the experts. The customer organization can focus its resources on only those areas that are critical to its own success.

4. Improvement in Supplier's Organization and Professional Skills

James C. Morgan, Applied Materials chief executive, declares, "No question. We learn more from our Japanese customers than we do from our American ones. That's beginning to change, but much of our success in the rest of the world comes from what we learn from *our best Japanese customers.*"

Suppliers benefit from the pressure world-class customers bring to bear to improve quality and deliveries. Sherwin Greenblatt, president of Bose, receives a monthly report card from his Japanese customers, Nissan and Toyota. Bose ships acoustics equipment that is installed by Nissan and Toyota in custom car sound systems and superior product quality is assumed. Timely deliveries are also demanded; when Bose misses a daily delivery goal, it is noted on the report card that Greenblatt receives. His intimate knowledge of his factory's quality performance and his customer's needs allows him to zero in on problem areas that will make Bose a better customer to its own suppliers—a three-tiered network of interdependent organizations.

Customer personnel learn more and bring new communications skills back to their own organizations when they spend time with suppliers. *The best way to learn new techniques is to teach them to someone else.* Representing a customer, explaining strategic objectives, product and process flows is also called "reverse marketing."

There is an added benefit for customers when they explain how the organization works and what is required to be successful: new opportunities appear when users map their own processes.

Back in the early eighties, before Honda captured pieces of Briggs and Stratton's engine market, the Wisconsin producer was burdened with a complex, lengthy World War II–era planning system characterized by forecast, planning, and purchasing activities that were "never really done." By the time the new forecast requirements had been broken down and analyzed, then transmitted to procurement for new purchase orders (a time span never less than six months), the next planning cycle had begun. Located at the tail end of the system, much like many customers, purchasing was hit with revisions to revisions. To demonstate the futility of this cycle, I mapped the process, starting at the very beginning of the planning exercise with the customer order backlog and, where the backlog dropped off, the forecast. The resulting three-foot-long map of Briggs's planning cycle, including time-to-complete for each of the individual steps, was a revelation to Briggs's materials planning personnel. Like the Rosetta stone, it was the *only* document that allowed very separate functions to understand what the fellow in the other building was doing, and how the latest batch of changes impacted on the people that "few loved, but all feared," the purchasing buyers.

Suppliers' pressure on customers to communicate and share will mount. However, just as there are strong internal barriers to excellence, it will be tough to break down customers' old buying behaviors.

BARRIERS TO ACHIEVING WORLD-CLASS CUSTOMER STATUS

Manufacturers in the United States cite several obstacles to forming very tight, legally binding relationships between suppliers and their customers. There are no *keiretsu* (Japanese industry groups) in the U.S. Antitrust and other legislation, coupled with government hesitation on industrial policy, prevents companies from forming tight legal arrangements that could be construed as price fixing cartels.

Other excuses for not adopting habits of collaboration inherent to good customers abound. It's easier to use leverage than to risk open discussions. A few corporate leaders like GM substitute clout for long-term quality and performance development. In the short term, GM's financial pros may pull enough pennies out of component parts cost to raise the company's debt rating, but when the company applies its considerable muscle to pressure its suppliers for more cost cuts, you can bet that in addition to cutting quality, suppliers will be looking to hire a new customer!

Good communications build trust. But communications can also create a barrier that blocks well-intentioned information-sharing efforts. Information systems should perform valuable communications work, but if the system is poorly designed or doesn't link well, customer-supplier partners will continue to be frustrated by an apparent communications problem, and genuine issues will be sidelined.

One adventuresome pharmaceutical producer is rumored to be spending $14 million to acquire and beta test an immense software application that will handle megadoses of old purchasing data protocol—shopping carts filled with "hernia reports," pounds of purchase orders and shop orders. Will the $14 million garner better customer-supplier collaboration? Sure it will—

between the software vendor and his eager customer installers. Computer planning systems are not always the way to develop better communications. Partners themselves have the responsibility to improve relationships and communications, and to build trust. Complex software administered before simplification opportunities have been mapped won't achieve these goals. But they certainly will keep people busy and create a strong illusion of activity.

WHAT IS A WORLD-CLASS CUSTOMER?

Excellent suppliers need excellent customers. Unfortunately, for many organizations, supplier development has only meant concentrating on improved quality and other "technical" aspects of partnering. Activities such as reducing the supplier base to more workable networks are only the first steps in forming partnerships.

For many manufacturers, customer partnerships focus only on product, e.g., product quality and product delivery schedules. But supply management encompasses new technology applications and production *processes*, like JIT and management behavior, as well.

Management behavior is always included in suppliers' lists of customer attributes. Usually suppliers mention honesty, ethics, and responsiveness. While these characteristics may seem difficult to translate into operating codes, organizations whose leaders model good practices know the difference. When Honda of America's Dave Nelson tells employees to invite suppliers to joint benchmarking conferences, saying "It's the right thing to do," he is setting an example that makes it easy for buyers to follow during daily activities.

In addition, Breakthrough Partnering requires excellent planning and control of materials plans and schedules, as well as superior quality and predictable delivery times. Good customers have characteristics that are genuinely beneficial to both parties, including:

- Awareness of and attentiveness to their suppliers' needs
- A track record of fulfilling promises made to suppliers
- Willingness to be open, to share forward plans with suppliers
- Willingness to explore process and product improvement suggestions at early stages of product development and all through a product's life
- A pattern of competent systems and processes required to make transactions with suppliers more effficient, such as Statistical Process Control and EDI
- Willingness to help the supplier develop and install competent systems and processes compatible with their own
- A pattern of providing quick responses to problems raised by suppliers
- Willingness to accept feedback from key suppliers on behavior in all functions that touch the supplier, and to initiate corrective action where required.

Xerox's description of the model customer includes many of these same characteristics, grouped into five key categories: management attitude, quality, cost, delivery, and service. Several fall into the challenge of communications.

Eastman Kodak and the Hoover Company are pioneering open partner communications, starting with their partnership document. Kodak has examined what suppliers and customers promise to deliver, and what they expect in return. Early involvement in the design and establishment of the customer's requirements, as well as improvement of their manufacturing processes, is included in the list of expectations of suppliers from Kodak.

Motorola conducts quarterly confidential surveys of its major suppliers to evaluate its performance as a customer. The survey instruments are designed by Motorola's market research department to minimize statistical bias. Each facility is rated at the plant level in nineteen areas that the company feels are important to the customer-supplier partnership (see Resource 4).

The company wants to concentrate purchases exclusively with world-class suppliers. As a customer, Motorola's adoption of its "Six Sigma" quality goal recognizes that the company needs a team effort to reach its goal. Suppliers are asked to reduce their cycle time, and deliver more quickly and dependably. And the customer expects suppliers to reduce their prices by sharing cost improvements resulting from better quality and shorter cycle time. Suppliers are "strongly encouraged" to compete for the Baldrige Award, a process that uncovers quality opportunities in a prescriptive manner.

Motorola's world-class customer approach began several years ago, when they asked their own customer service and production control personnel, "Who is a good customer?" Since then, even though the questions are now posed to external suppliers, the company continues to update its definition of a world-class customer.

Honda of America has added the AME Customer Survey to its partnering techniques. Recognizing that a good supplier audit and development program is still only half the picture, the company surveyed all 246 of its suppliers to find out whether HAM was consistently behaving as a good customer and where it could improve. (See Resource 5.)

Each supplier survey was reviewed by the vice president of purchasing who looked for patterns in the responses, as well as individual recommendations. Two comments were assigned to continuous improvement teams for action:

- Suppliers wanted one "window person," rather than several different contacts.
- Honda's policy of growing the people and the company includes job rotations. Less rotation makes suppliers' jobs easier.

Three other organizations use the AME customer-supplier survey: Harley Davidson, McNeil Consumer Laboratories, and Becton Dickinson. Each company emphasizes that suppliers must be assured that actions will be taken as a result of their feedback. Without that commitment, customer credibility drops. Two of McNeil's suppliers, National Label and Mallinckrodt Specialty Chemicals, urged that customers pay attention to financial terms, as well as design and delivery issues. The repeated, regular administration of the survey helps customers spot trends, especially during high-growth or restructuring periods, when the survey becomes a baseline.

Solectron uses weekly administration of the CSI Customer Satisfaction Index to improve customer-supplier partnerships. (See Resource 1.)

Customers frequently attend production meetings, and Solectron's Tuesday-Wednesday-Thursday meeting sequence dedicates one day to customer feedback.

BECOMING A WORLD-CLASS CUSTOMER

Ken Stork, former Motorola director of materials and purchasing, notes that there are significant differences between the average and excellent customer.

- World-class customers solicit information on defects the customer must correct.
- They truly buy on the basis of total cost, including administrative, process, quality, and other costs, not invoicing price.
- Actual procurement behavior coincides with the printed policies and procedures documentation.
- "Same face," a fourth characteristic of world-class customers, means that no matter where the supplier touches the organization, whether it is engineering, or accounts payable, or materials and production, the message is the same. Suppliers hate to

get the runaround or different stories from different customer functions. They want to hear the same message repeated in the same language. Stated policies and day-to-day activities should match. There should be no gap between, say, what the procedures manual proscribes for supplier selection, and the way buyers trim down the supply base.

When a supplier representative calls on purchasing buyers, the answers they receive on new product specifications and required manufacturing tolerances should be identical to the information that's given to the engineering design group—Honda's *Kintori Amay* or "same face" philosophy in action.

Becoming a world-class customer is difficult work. If a customer chooses to work on only half the partnership—supplier development, for example—the partnering results will be, predictably, limited.

FOUR ACTION STEPS TO BECOMING A WORLD-CLASS CUSTOMER

1. Ask them.

Listen for clear signals. World-class customers practice listening. They frequently ask suppliers how they are doing as a customer. Motorola's periodic supplier surveys not only pinpoint areas needing improvement, they establish a baseline for ongoing partnership monitoring. Because surveys aren't taken every day, their use needs to be carefully weighed and executed. In fact, preparation for a customer survey, and follow-through, especially disposition of confidential data, is as important as the survey questions. Where any opportunity for misuse of survey data exists, or where a supplier would be intimidated into answering unobjectively, a third-party should mail and collate results to protect respondents and guarantee honest responses.

2. *Tell them.*

Share important information. Honda shares designs, schedules, cost data, and special topic information with suppliers. All communication vehicles need review. Evaluate all paperwork routinely initiated or processed by purchasing customers for usefulness. Purchase orders can be replaced with blanket orders (cut infrequently, covering generally long-term agreements) and weekly schedules of JIT anticipated usage transmitted electronically. Invoice preparation and comparison to shipping documents and open orders can be streamlined. Xerox, for example, has stopped sending Bechtel paper invoices prepared for each individual purchase order. Instead, Bechtel's preference for electronic billing once a month has replaced the daily paperwork shuffling.[2]

3. *Invite them.*

Invest in relationships. Supplier councils, supplier recognition days, joint benchmarking forums, and other open-door activities build trust. Other innovative customer practices build trust and improve communications.

Honda's BP (Best Partner) program, representing sixty suppliers, is a systematic approach to supplier development from which only two suppliers have dropped out. In exchange for supplier resources, time, effort, and commitment, Honda dedicates one or two of its professionals to working with suppliers who sign on for the program. Honda sent people to help in a small Mexican electronics assembly facility that at several points had been a problem supplier. The Honda people surprised everyone by locating on the production floor. Their first activity, to pick up a broom and clean up the area, was unexpected. The Best Partner program continued for thirteen weeks, at a total cost to Honda of about $100,000 in meals, travel, and missed time for two Honda pros. The *smallest* productivity gain achieved by this level of investment with sixty participating suppliers has been 21 percent.

4. Work with Them.

Work together. When the distinctions between customer and supplier partners begin to blur, customer-supplier partnership teams take on the appearance of a virtual company, a new organization formed with elements of all contributing partners. In fact, when one of Boeing's initial project teams, having reached the end of one product design phase, regrouped with new members, there was a natural letdown for departing members. For them, this experience was one of the best of their careers, one whose intensity produced a high that they were not ready to surrender. According to Rick Mayo, head of Honda's Best Partner program, working together on site is the best and preferred way to train supplier personnel. Mayo tells supplier employees and management, "We aren't going to do it. *You're* going to do it, or we'll leave."

The world-class customer concept is an idea whose time has come. As anyone knows, whoever gets to market first wins. Enlightened customers need to work proactively with suppliers early. And the customer is the member of the partnership that must take the initiative and work at trustbuilding.

Building good internal habits of collaboration and communication takes time and practice, but it is a prerequisite for taking down the barriers to good external partnering. Leaders such as Motorola and Honda are systematically developing their supplier base, and winning market share because of it. The mechanics for starting relationship building are here—Motorola's Supplier Survey and the AME Customer Supplier Survey. While the identification of customer problem areas is vital, how companies respond to the data is more important. When suppliers consistently see ethical and mutually beneficial improvement practices on the part of their customers, they naturally perform better. When they don't, they behave accordingly. You always get what you pay for.

NOTES

1. Michael Schrage, "Innovation," *Boston Globe*, June 23, 1991. The quote at the beginning of the chapter was also taken from this article.

2. Claudia Deutsch, "Stronger Ties with Customer Make Sense," *New York Times*, Febuary 20, 1991.

CHAPTER 11

Partnering for Enterprise Advantage—Innovation and Growth

*"T*hey bought it."

One GM supplier went seven rounds negotiating and renegotiating its "contract"—prices, quantities, and delivery schedules—with the Detroit Giant and survived. Showing me "The Purchasing Vice," a well-worn fax of purported instructions from GM to its purchasing managers, the supplier noted that his company experienced "everything in it ["The Purchasing Vice"] as we went through the seven-round negotiation process."

The document outlines how to leverage a smaller "partner" for short-term results. Among its recommendations are to warm up suppliers to obtain information, lie to them if necessary, and exert various other "terror tactics" to keep them in a leveraged position. The list describes how *not* to cement long-term partnerships:

- Offer exaggerated growth projections.
- Establish very early long-term contract rules but do not negotiate in detail.
- Resist all suggestions that some costs are controllable and others are not (e.g., materials).

- Focus all activity on reducing the immediate price dramatically.
- Destabilize the supplier with repeated meetings and "urgent" demands for information.
- Set deadlines for suppliers to meet but increase anxiety by deferring decisions.
- Tie up the short-term price, but keep nibbling at the eleventh hour.

It's hard to argue short-term vs. long-term partnering techniques in a financially weakened institution. Stockholder, union, and internal pressures take over. The results of this leveraged procurement approach have been demonstrated: The customer will squeeze little more than price cuts from the supplier experts on whom their future depends, and suppliers will seek out new customers.

Not every partnership is born of a near catastrophe. Certainly companies like Honda of America, Motorola, Xyplex, Apple, Hewlett-Packard, Sun and many others have discovered, in the words of Dave Nelson, that "it was the right thing to do." A range of companies practicing partnering the right way have shown the positive results of doing it that way. Most of these stories boil down to communications and trust. Technical issues like EDI need to be addressed as part of the communications linkages, of course, but electronic linkages do not guarantee good alliances. Breakthrough Partnering is not achieved by stringing wires together. Through each of the success stories run four common threads:

1. *Executive-level commitment to, or engagement in, the partnership process.* Seagate's participation in the EMC partnership would not have been 100 percent without the support and vision of Seagate Chairman Al Shugart; neither would the Molex-Motorola partnership have thrived without the active support of Molex President John Krehbiel, Jr.

2. *Communications.* The winners ensure that touchpoints are in place. Procurement professionals must be strong communicators, equally comfortable at the blackboard and delivering difficult messages one-on-one.

Included in the broad topic of communications are customer-supplier assessment and feedback tools like Solectron's Customer Satisfaction Index (CSI), the Motorola Quality System Review (QSR), the Williams Technologies Customer Rating Sheet, and the AME Customer Survey. These are not just quality barometers. To be effective they must be dynamic, iterative communications tools, used first as a benchmark, and then in regular improvement meetings as diagnostic improvement aids.

3. *Protocol.* Without a protocol, such as Boeing's Statement of Partnership agreement, teams find themselves on the field without a rulebook. Protocol questions must be resolved before the team starts training. Making up the rules as you go along won't work here.

4. *Strong partners prepared to participate in a team effort.* The profile of the new procurement professional is someone who is multiskilled, a team player, and a superb communicator. These skills can be developed and enhanced with positive role models, opportunities for practice, and further development available in training programs like Motorola University and the Nypro Institute.

Even when individuals acquire skills, however, strong partnerships will only flourish in a supportive environment. Specifically, hierarchies with limited individual decision-making, no team projects, communication through memo, complex MIS systems, and other structural barriers will not optimize individual partner potential.

KEY SUPPLIERS NEED A PLACE AT THE TABLE

EMC and Seagate Technologies turned their partnership around by taking financial objectives and translating them into daily partnership operating activities. Traditional buying and selling practices wouldn't work here. Steve Greenspan, Seagate's newly appointed senior vice president of corporate quality and customer service, prepared for his first meeting with customer EMC by packing five inches of slides into his briefcase: He was ready to sell. Mike Schoonover, leader of the EMC team, responded, "No thank you, we have our own slides." Three hours later, says Valerie Ellsworth, Seagate vice president of strategic sales, "Steve looked at the customer, put his slides away, and said 'I got it' "—namely, that the *partnership* wasn't going to be based on *selling*, but on *mutually* beneficial customer and supplier activities.

To become EMC's premier supplier, both Seagate *and EMC* had to practice a number of challenging Breakthrough Partnering skills, 90 percent of which hinged on communications. Indeed, the delivery of the first message, says Seagate's Ellsworth, was the hardest part of the relationship. "If Seagate was going to be the supplier, the company needed to not only embrace the customer's quality demands—one million hours mean time between failures—but *deliver it now, right away*."

The customer performed several tasks extremely well. First, EMC did their homework, and came to what could have been a sales presentation ready to demand solutions to their core problems. The company specifically outlined what its corporate goals and objectives were, and what actions they would need to take in order to be successful. And based on that outline, the status quo was unacceptable. "Good enough" wasn't good enough any longer. EMC recognized that its suppliers would directly impact their success, and thus disclosed the results of their new corporate focus to each of their suppliers, presenting them with the challenge and the opportunity to make EMC successful.

The customer gave Seagate "a place at the table." EMC linked Seagate intricately to its lines of communication, making it what Seagate executives described as "a true business partner." The supplier was invited to be a part of discussions on corporate goals and objectives, market direction, and product planning. EMC gave Seagate unlimited access to the engineers designing the products, eliminated many layers of bureaucracy, and repeatedly involved Seagate in discussions of what it needed to be successful.

Secondly, both partners focused on real issues that would have a direct impact on how they, *the partners*, were going to make the customer more profitable and more successful in the marketplace. This was not a fuzzy discussion about scorecards and good intentions; the issues could be easily translated to how they were going to make EMC more competitive. Improvements went beyond information sharing to joint technical testing, detailed process changes that improved product design and reliability.

MAKING THE MOVE TO LONG-TERM PARTNERING

Some companies deny their suppliers a "place at the table." They provide limited input on their programs, request suppliers to "just deliver," and thereby limit the opportunities to take advantage of the synergy of the two companies' capabilities and product efficiencies. Breakthrough Partnering presents a powerful challenge to traditional purchasing practices. Overused terms like "culture change" and "paradigm shift" only partially describe the impact on an organization of making the move to long-term partnerships.

You can use this book as the starting point to making that move; the Resource Section offers tools to throw into the toolkit. The excellence models provide inspiration, and they have been more than generous and willing to share their Breakthrough Partnership experience. And the "bad boys" show how not to attempt partnering.

All six supports of the Breakthrough Partnership Bridge can be built by individuals and teams in the right environment. Without the Seven Breakthrough Partnership Drivers, companies will fail to realize the full potential of collective enterprise advantage. With them, the possibilities are unlimited.

Dave Nelson, whose roots extend back to a farm in Southern Indiana, told this story at a Honda supplier development conference:

> A visitor from California noticed cows nibbling on the green shoots of an abundant plant on a farm in Indiana. Although this plant, called Johnson grass, looked good, it was a crop destroyer. Every few years farmers had to plow their fields under to stop its growth. The visitor wrote back to his Indiana host asking how he could get some of that lovely plant started at home, to which the farmer sent an envelope containing a single seed and instructions:
>
> > Take this seed, drop it in the
> > ground, and run like hell!

Breakthrough Partnering is contagious because it allows partners to produce the very best products they can and to realize more than they imagined possible by drawing on the skills of "the experts"—the partners they have chosen to join their team. Breakthrough Partnering offers the small and medium-sized company all the power of the larger enterprise; for the large organization, it offers a methodology to acquire innovation, growth, and flexibility.

The Resource Section

The tools included in this section are simple aids to help companies partner better. Breakthrough Partnering emphasizes the importance of preparing *internally* to be a good partner. The Competitive Management Capabilities Survey and the AME Meeting Evaluation are good tools to enforce deliberate management of internal processes.

Use the AME Customer Survey to become a better partner; modify is to fit your supplier base, to protect respondents' confidentiality, and to establish a baseline to monitor progress. The Motorola and Solectron documents are equally well suited for strengthening customer-supplier communications.

This Breakthrough Partnering Resource Section contains the following documents:

Resource 1: Solectron Customer Satisfaction Index (CSI)

Resource 2: Competitive Management Capabilities Survey

Resource 3a: Williams Technologies Performance Matrix ("Customer grades us this way")

Resource 3b: GM Powertrain Customer Evaluation ("We grade customers this way")

Resource 4: Motorola Supplier Evaluation of Customers

Resource 5: AME Customer Survey

Resource 6: AME Meeting Evaluation

Resource 7: Partnership Diagnostic

Solectron Customer Satisfaction Index (CSI)

Solectron Customer Satisfaction Index (CSI)

October 12, 1992

Judy Smith
Mountain View, CA

Dear Judy:

Solectron is interested in your perceptions of your
relationship with them. The attached questionnaire outlines
several important elements of that relationship. We would
appreciate your feedback. Your name and the name of your
company will be kept confidential by Questions, Inc.

We will call you tomorrow to note your responses in a brief
telephone conversation. Or feel free to fax it back to us at
xxx-xxxx.

If you have any questions, please call me at xxx-xxxx.
Thank you for your assistance.

Sincerely,
Erica Leyton
Project Manager

SOLECTRON
Supplier Relationship Questionnaire

<u>Communication</u>

1. How effectively does Solectron communicate its goals, directions and expectations ?

2. How would you evaluate Solectron's openness to feedback and suggestions for improvement, as well as their willingness to escalate issues to senior management for review?

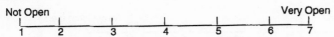

3. How accessible are Solectron's procurement personnel in terms of their willingness to return phone calls, faxes, etc.?

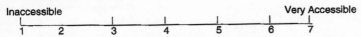

4. How would you evaluate the consistency in direction between Corporate Material and Division Material?

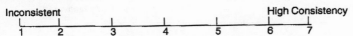

5. What one thing would you recommend to improve communication at Solectron?

_____

<u>Business Processes</u>

6. How would you compare Solectron's Supplier Performance Measurement process to the process utilized by other companies?

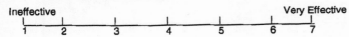

Solectron Customer Satisfaction Index (CSI)

7. How would you describe the visibility of Solectron/Customer schedule requirements?

8. How would you evaluate Solectron's fairness in the negotiation and business award process?

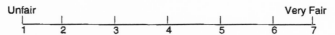

9. What is the commitment of Solectron's senior management to supplier relationships?

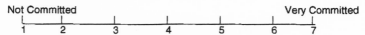

10. How would you describe Solectron's approach to supplier relationships?

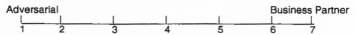

11. What initiative does Solectron take in driving improvements in quality and overall performance?

12. To what degree does Solectron facilitate early supplier involvement between itself, suppliers and customers?

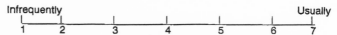

13. How cost effective is it to support Solectron's procurement organizational structure?

Solectron Customer Satisfaction Index (CSI)

14. To what degree does Solectron add value between its suppliers and customers?

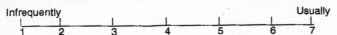

Infrequently / Usually — scale 1–7

15. How would you describe Solectron's professionalism and ethics?

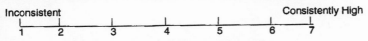

Inconsistent / Consistently High — scale 1–7

16. How effectively does Solectron identify problem areas?

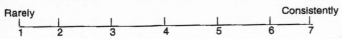

Rarely / Consistently — scale 1–7

17. What one thing would you recommend to improve business process at Solectron?

Competitive Analysis

18. How would you compare Solectron to other contract manufacturers?

    S=Solectron   O=Other Contract Manufacturers

Please place the appropriate initial for Solectron (S) and other contract manufacturers (O) by the number you designate on the scale.

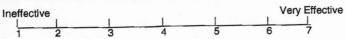

Ineffective / Very Effective — scale 1–7

19. How would you compare Solectron to your best customer?

    B=Best Customer   S=Solectron

Please place the appropriate initial by the number you designate on the scale.

Ineffective / Very Effective — scale 1–7

Courtesy of Solectron.

Competitive Management Capabilities Survey

Competitive Management Capabilities Survey

Competitive Management Capabilities Survey

Instructions: Answer all questions, leaving none blank. Use your best understanding of the meaning of the terms used in this instrument in making your response. For each competency listed in the center of the page:
a) On the left, circle the number that indicates how important each competency is for managers to possess in executing the corporate competitive strategy for the future;
b) On the right, circle the number that indicates current organizational capabilities or strengths in each competency area.

Skill area's relative importance to execution of company's strategy:					The ability to:	Company's current relative strength in this skill area:				
No Importance			**High Importance**			**Very Weak**			**Very Strong**	
A. 1	2	3	4	5	Manage Strategic Change	1	2	3	4	5
B. 1	2	3	4	5	Manage Cultural Change	1	2	3	4	5
C. 1	2	3	4	5	Articulate a Tangible Vision	1	2	3	4	5
D. 1	2	3	4	5	Exhibit a High Degree of Integrity	1	2	3	4	5
E. 1	2	3	4	5	Communicate Corporate Values	1	2	3	4	5
F. 1	2	3	4	5	Communicate Effectively	1	2	3	4	5
G. 1	2	3	4	5	Interface with Global Counterparts	1	2	3	4	5
H. 1	2	3	4	5	Understand Global Economic, Political, Cultural, Social Issues	1	2	3	4	5
I. 1	2	3	4	5	Be Flexible and Adaptive	1	2	3	4	5
J. 1	2	3	4	5	Manage Flexible Organizations	1	2	3	4	5
K. 1	2	3	4	5	Be a Team Leader	1	2	3	4	5
L. 1	2	3	4	5	Be a Team Member	1	2	3	4	5
M. 1	2	3	4	5	Manage Innovation	1	2	3	4	5
N. 1	2	3	4	5	Synthesize Complex Information	1	2	3	4	5
O. 1	2	3	4	5	Learn How to Learn	1	2	3	4	5
P. 1	2	3	4	5	Think Integratively	1	2	3	4	5
Q. 1	2	3	4	5	Demonstrate Effective Political Skills	1	2	3	4	5
R. 1	2	3	4	5	Influence Others Without Authority	1	2	3	4	5
S. 1	2	3	4	5	Negotiate for Resources	1	2	3	4	5
T. 1	2	3	4	5	Manage Ethnically/Culturally Diverse Workforce	1	2	3	4	5
U. 1	2	3	4	5	Exhibit a Strong Customer Orientation	1	2	3	4	5
V. 1	2	3	4	5	Build Customer/Supplier Alliances	1	2	3	4	5
W. 1	2	3	4	5	Manage a Fast Cycle Organization	1	2	3	4	5
X. 1	2	3	4	5	Manage a Leaner Organization	1	2	3	4	5
Y. 1	2	3	4	5	Manage Quality Improvement	1	2	3	4	5
Z. 1	2	3	4	5	Embrace New Technologies	1	2	3	4	5
AA. 1	2	3	4	5	Manage Strategy to Action/Results	1	2	3	4	5
BB. 1	2	3	4	5	Take Risks/Initiative	1	2	3	4	5
CC. 1	2	3	4	5	Develop and Coach Others	1	2	3	4	5
DD. 1	2	3	4	5	Structure Developmental Job Assignments	1	2	3	4	5
EE. 1	2	3	4	5	Manage a Staff Re-Skilling Effort	1	2	3	4	5
FF. 1	2	3	4	5	Plan for Changing Human Resource Requirements	1	2	3	4	5
GG. 1	2	3	4	5	Make Future Oriented Staffing Decisions	1	2	3	4	5
HH. 1	2	3	4	5	Demonstrate Excellence in Functional Management	1	2	3	4	5
II. 1	2	3	4	5	Have Knowledge of the Total Business	1	2	3	4	5
JJ. 1	2	3	4	5	Demonstrate Competence in Financial Management	1	2	3	4	5
KK. 1	2	3	4	5	Demonstrate Competence in Information Systems	1	2	3	4	5

Please list 2-3 additional leadership competencies that will be crucial to competitive success:

Excerpted from Patricia E. Moody, "Workforce Development," *Target*, January–February 1993, Reprinted with permission.

Williams Technologies Performance Matrix ("Customer grades us this way")

Williams Technologies Performance Matrix

Williams Technologies Performance Matrix ("customer grades us this way....")													
Quality							Inventory	Performance to Contract			Other		
Warranty 6 Month Exposure 3 Month Average	Warranty W.T + 1/2 Shared Liability	Final Test %	Sediment Mg/unit	Teardown Average Defects/ 5 Transmissions	Leak Test Accept Rate	Cont. Improv	Turns Per Year	Customer Response Reports	Drive Audit (Units)	Root Cause	Case Usage Rate	Scale	
5.66%	18.30%	95.44%	155.1	6.25	99.60%	*10	11.8	100.00%	18.0	5.00%	94.90%		
3.00%	16.50%	97.50%	240.0	0.00	100.00%	10	21.0	100.00%	20.0	5.00%	98.00%	10	
3.50%	18.00%	97.00%	248.0	2.00	99.75%	9	19.0	90.00%	19.0	4.80%	97.50%	9	
4.00%	19.50%	96.50%	256.0	4.00	99.50%	8	17.0	80.00%	18.0	4.60%	97.00%	8	
4.50%	21.00%	96.00%	264.0	6.00	99.25%	7	15.0	70.00%	17.0	4.40%	96.50%	7	
5.00%	22.50%	95.50%	272.0	8.00	99.00%	6	13.0	60.00%	16.0	4.20%	96.00%	6	
5.50%	24.00%	95.00%	280.0	10.00	98.75%	5	11.0	50.00%	15.0	4.00%	95.50%	5	
6.00%	25.50%	94.40%	288.0	12.00	98.50%	4	9.0	40.00%	14.0	3.80%	95.00%	4	
6.50%	27.00%	94.00%	296.0	14.00	98.25%	3	7.0	30.00%	13.0	3.60%	94.50%	3	
7.00%	28.50%	93.50%	304.0	16.00	98.00%	2	5.0	20.00%	12.0	3.40%	94.00%	2	
7.50%	30.00%	93.00%	312.0	18.00	97.75%	1	3.0	10.00%	11.0	3.20%	93.50%	1	
4	8	5	10	6	8	10	5	10	8	10	3	87	Score
6	12	5	14	14	5	14	8	5	5	5	7	100	Weight
24	96	25	140	84	40	140	40	50	40	50	21	750	Value

Targets For Excellence 1.5 **Target = 0 Discrepancies** **Month June 92** **750**

4T60/4T60-E Performance Matrix, FWD Service Product Team

(1) SRTA WARRANTY — Hard part (R7000) claims only.
Claims per 100 vehicles with 6 months exposure. Last 3 months running average from GM Corporation Warranty Date.

(2) WARRANTY LIABILITY
Claims per 100 analyzed returns. 100% SRTA site liability + 50% shared (SRTA site + GMPD) liability.

(3) FINAL TEST %
Acceptance rate of final test machines at SRTA site.
[(Monthly total accepted units/by monthly total tested units) x 100].

(4) SEDIMENT (Mg/unit)
From monthly audit performed at GMPT plant by reliability.

(5) TEARDOWN (Average defects/5 transmissions)
From monthly teardown audits performed at GM Powertrain plant. Discrepancies are reported for mis-builds and low torque applications.
[(Disc./# units audited) x 5].

(6) LEAK TEST ACCEPT RATE %
Acceptance rate of leak test machines at SRTA site.
[(Monthly total of accepted units divided by monthly total of tested units) x 100].

(7) CONTINUOUS IMPROVEMENT
2 points maximum given to each of the following categories:
Quality — Charts and 5-phase reports updated monthly.
Gauging — Gauges certified and records up to date.
V.I.P.S. — Shipped on time (24 hours).
Job Instructions — Written procedures updated and on job. Preventative maintenance schedules followed.
Cost/Unit — Total cost of Material, Freight, and Labor/units produced.

(8) TURNS PER YEAR — GOAL = 20 TURNS PER YEAR (obsolete parts exc)
TURNS = (cost of material used in month) x 12
(beginning inventory value for months)

(9) CUSTOMER RESPONSIVENESS
Reports and requests submitted on time.

(10) DRIVE AUDITS (Units/Month)
The number of units driven divided by the number units produced. Based on 1.3 units per day. Score excludes Allante models.

(11) ROOT CAUSE
Five percent of remanufacturing production analyzed in root cause.

(12) CASE USAGE RATE
The number of transmission cases scrapped divided by the number unit accepted. Number reported is three-month running average.

Courtesy of Williams Technologies.

GM Powertrain Customer Evaluation ("We grade customers this way")

GM Powertrain Customer Evaluation

GM Powertrain 4T60 SRTA Customer Evaluation ("we grade customers this way...")								
Schedule	Parts Delivery	New Parts Quality	<None> Synchronous	Communications	Price/Cost	Customer Supplier Relationship	Scale	
10	10	10	10	10	10	10	10	
9	9	9	9	9	9	9	9	
8	8	8	8	8	8	8	8	
7	7	7	7	7	7	7	7	
6	6	6	6	6	6	6	6	
5	5	5	5	5	5	5	5	
4	4	4	4	4	4	4	4	
3	3	3	3	3	3	3	3	
2	2	2	2	2	2	2	2	
1	1	1	1	1	1	1	1	
9	8	7	6	10	9	8	57	Score
15	10	15	20	10	20	10	100	Weight
135	80	105	120	100	180	80	800	Value

| Goal 1000 | | | | Month June 1992 | | Score 800 | | |

Points of Measure

ITEM # 1 SCHEDULE
- Schedule in multiple of truckload (104)
- No fluctuation in given month (freeze volume)
- No variation in mix per week
- No VIP's
- Communicate schedule EDI
  A change in either of these would cost one point.

10 = Above
9 = Any one (1) change
8 = Any two (2) changes
7 = Any three (3) changes
6 = Any four (4) changes
5 = Any five (5) changes
0-4 = THANKFUL FOR BUSINESS

ITEM # 2 PARTS DELIVERY
10 = JIT and Kanban, all delivered
9 = Some JIT, all delivered
8 = Smooth but large quantities
7 = Back order in 2nd week of schedule
6 = Late (1)
5 = Late (2)
4 = Late (3)
3 = Back order in current week
2 = Subassembly down
1 = Part of final assembly line down
0 = LINE DOWN

ITEM # 3 NEW PARTS QUALITY
10 = Ready for new line — ZERO defects
9 = < 5% need inspection or clean

8 = GCN resolution outstanding over 30 days
7 = 15% parts needed inspection or clean
6 = 20% parts needed inspection or clean
5 = GCN resolution outstanding over 60 days
4 = 25% parts needed inspection or clean
3 = GCN resolution outstanding 6 months
2 = Subassembly went down
1 = Part of final assembly line went down
0 = LINE DOWN

ITEM # 4 SYNCHRONOUS
10 = SIT has followed all ten (10) steps to Synchronous mix
9 = Demonstrates eighteen (18) characteristics
8 = Producing mutual cost reductions
7 =
6 = Treats supplier as partner
5 = Implemented some elements of Synchronous with supplier
4 =
3 = Just getting started/learning
2 = Can spell SYNCHRONOUS
1 = Can say SYNCHRONOUS (syn' chro' nous)
0 = Not moving toward SYNCHRONOUS

ITEM # 5 COMMUNICATIONS
10 = No surprises, responsive and all information on time
9 = Any one (1) surprise
8 = Any two (2) surprises
7 = Any three (3) surprises
6 = Any four (4) surprises
5 = Heard it from truck driver
4 = Information showed up in mail or fax

3 =
2 =
1 =
0 = Heard from another SRTA site

ITEM # 6 PRICE/COST
10 = Pays a fair price; helps reduce cost
9 =
8 = Mechanism in place to identify additional costs and adjust price
7 =
6 =
5 =
4 =
3 =
2 =
1 =
0 = Beats supplier for every last penny

ITEM # 7 CUSTOMER/SUPPLIER RELATIONSHIP
10 = Partnership that mutually benefits both
9 = Aids growth — supplier rationalization — new business
8 = Establishes two way performance matrix
7 =
6 =
5 = Considers supplier a commodity
4 =
3 =
2 =
1 =
0 = Supplier = a vendor

Courtesy of Williams Technologies.

Motorola Supplier Evaluation of Customers

Motorola Supplier Evaluation of Customers

I   Please check the box corresponding to the annual dollar volume of business you do with each of the six Motorola facilities listed.

II   Please rate each **Motorola** facility with which you do more than $25,000 in business annually on each of the following areas. Circle one number on the scale from 1 to 6, where **1 is Poor and 6 is Excellent.**

I   **ANNUAL BUSINESS VOLUME WITH:**

	PLANT 1	PLANT 2	PLANT 3
No Business With	☐	☐	☐
Less Than $25,000	☐	☐	☐
$25,000 - $100,000	☐	☐	☐
$101,000 - $250,000	☐	☐	☐
$251,000 - $500,000	☐	☐	☐
More Than $500,000	☐	☐	☐

II   **EVALUATION:**

A. TECHNICAL, ENGINEERING AND QUALITY:

		PLANT 1	PLANT 2	PLANT 3
1.	Technical Support	1 2 3 4 5 6	1 2 3 4 5 6	1 2 3 4 5 6
2.	Technology Sharing	1 2 3 4 5 6	1 2 3 4 5 6	1 2 3 4 5 6
3.	Quality Initiatives	1 2 3 4 5 6	1 2 3 4 5 6	1 2 3 4 5 6
4.	Cost Reduction Response	1 2 3 4 5 6	1 2 3 4 5 6	1 2 3 4 5 6
5.	Identifying Cost Drivers	1 2 3 4 5 6	1 2 3 4 5 6	1 2 3 4 5 6
6.	Prints & Specifications	1 2 3 4 5 6	1 2 3 4 5 6	1 2 3 4 5 6
7.	Early Supplier Involvement	1 2 3 4 5 6	1 2	1 2 3 4 5 6

B. SUPPLIER SELECTION AND DEVELOPMENT:

		PLANT 1	PLANT 2	PLANT 3
8.	Purchasing Professionalism	1 2 3 4 5 6	1 2 3 4 5 6	1 2 3 4 5 6
9.	Professionalism in Conducting Supplier Surveys	1 2 3 4 5 6	1 3 4 5 6	1 2 3 4 5 6
10.	Training and Education Effectiveness	1 2 3 4 5 6	1 2 3 4 5 6	1 2 3 4 5 6
11.	Commodity Management	1 2 3 4 5	2 3 4 5 6	1 2 3 4 5 6
12.	Adherence to Policies, Procedures and Ethics	1 2 3 4 5 6	1 2 3 4 5 6	1 2 3 4 5 6
13.	Negotiation/Award Process	1 2 3 4	1 2 3 4 5 6	1 2 3 4 5 6

C. SUPPLIER PARTNERSHIP:

		PLANT 1	PLANT 2	PLANT 3
14.	PFG Process	1 2 3 4 5 6	1 2 3 4 5 6	1 2 3 4 5 6
15.	Schedule Sharing	1 2 3 4 5 6	1 2 3 4 5 6	1 2 3 4 5 6
16.	Schedule Quality	1 2 3 4 5 6	1 2 3 4 5 6	1 2 3 4 5 6
17.	Business Growth Potential	1 2 3 4 5 6	1 2 3 4 5 6	1 2 3 4 5 6
18.	Improved Performance	1 2 3 4 5 6	1 2 3 4 5 6	1 2 3 4 5 6
19.	Communications/Feedback	1 2 3 4 5 6	1 2 3 4 5 6	1 2 3 4 5 6
20.	Preferred Status	1 2 3 4 5 6	1 2 3 4 5 6	1 2 3 4 5 6
21.	Management Commitment to Partnership	1 2 3 4 5 6	1 2 3 4 5 6	1 2 3 4 5 6
22.	Purchasing Commitment to Partnership	1 2 3 4 5 6	1 2 3 4 5 6	1 2 3 4 5 6
23.	Engineering Commitment to Partnership	1 2 3 4 5 6	1 2 3 4 5 6	1 2 3 4 5 6
24.	Payment Terms	1 2 3 4 5 6	1 2 3 4 5 6	1 2 3 4 5 6

D. SUMMARY:

		PLANT 1	PLANT 2	PLANT 3
25.	Overall Rating	1 2 3 4 5 6	1 2 3 4 5 6	1 2 3 4 5 6
26.	Recent Trend	1 2 3 4 5 6	1 2 3 4 5 6	1 2 3 4 5 6
27.	Business Continuation	1 2 3 4 5 6	1 2 3 4 5 6	1 2 3 4 5 6

Motorola Supplier Evaluation of Customers

III Finally, **excluding Motorola**, please consider your best customer in each category and rate that company from 1 to 6, with **1 being Poor and 6 being Excellent**, for that category by circling one number. If no other customers are involved with your company in one or more of the areas listed, please indicate so by checking the box below "Does Not Apply". Space is provided to list "Best Customer" in each area if you wish to do so.

		Best In Category	Does Not Apply	Best Customer (Name)
A.	**TECHNICAL, ENGINEERING AND QUALITY:**			
1.	Technical Support	1 2 3 4 5 6	☐	_____
2.	Technology Sharing	1 2 3 4 5 6	☐	_____
3.	Quality Initiatives	1 2 3 4 5 6	☐	_____
4.	Cost Reduction Response	1 2 3 4 5 6	☐	_____
5.	Identifying Cost Drivers	1 2 3 4 5 6	☐	_____
6.	Prints & Specifications	1 2 3 4 5 6	☐	_____
7.	Early Supplier Involvement	1 2 3 4 5 6	☐	_____
B.	**SUPPLIER SELECTION AND DEVELOPMENT:**			
8.	Purchasing Professionalism	1 2 3 4 5 6	☐	_____
9.	Professionalism in Conducting Supplier Surveys	1 2 3 4 5 6	☐	_____
10.	Training and Education Effectiveness	1 2 3 4 5 6	☐	_____
11.	Commodity Management	1 2 3 4 5 6	☐	_____
12.	Adherence to Policies, Procedures and Ethics	1 2 3 4 5 6	☐	_____
13.	Negotiation/Award Process	1 2 3 4 5 6	☐	_____
C.	**SUPPLIER PARTNERSHIP:**			
14.	PFG Process	1 2 3 4 5 6	☐	_____
15.	Schedule Sharing	1 2 3 4 5 6	☐	_____
16.	Schedule Quality	1 2 3 4 5 6	☐	_____
17.	Business Growth Potential	1 2 3 4 5 6	☐	_____
18.	Improved Performance	1 2 3 4 5 6	☐	_____
19.	Communications/Feedback	1 2 3 4 5 6	☐	_____
20.	Preferred Status	1 2 3 4 5 6	☐	_____
21.	Management Commitment to Partnership	1 2 3 4 5 6	☐	_____
22.	Purchasing Commitment to Partnership	1 2 3 4 5 6	☐	_____
23.	Engineering Commitment to Partnership	1 2 3 4 5 6	☐	_____
24.	Payment Terms	1 2 3 4 5 6	☐	_____
D.	**SUMMARY:**			
25.	Overall Rating	1 2 3 4 5 6	☐	_____
26.	Recent Trend	1 2 3 4 5 6	☐	_____
27.	Business Continuation	1 2 3 4 5 6	☐	_____

SAMPLE

Motorola Supplier Evaluation of Customers

My company participates in the following Motorola Partnership Programs:

	YES	NO
COMMODITY MANAGEMENT TEAM	☐	☐
SCHEDULE SHARING	☐	☐
EARLY SUPPLIER INVOLVEMENT	☐	☐

We strongly encourage you to use the space below to give us one or two ideas or suggestions for improvement.   You may use the blank page if necessary.

Space for issues or comments.   Use blank page if necessary.

It is **not necessary** to identify your name or company. However, if you care to do so or would like for me to follow-up or get back to you on any of the points or suggestions, you may fill in the following:

NAME:	
COMPANY	
ADDRESS:	
CITY/STATE/ZIP:	
TELEPHONE:	

Thank you for your time and valued input. Each and every idea will be evaluated and given serious consideration. Please know that your comments and suggestions are welcome at any time and can be forwarded to me at the address, telephone or fax numbers shown on the cover sheet.

AREAS OF CUSTOMER/SUPPLIER PARTNERSHIP DESCRIPTIONS

A. Technical, Engineering and Quality:

1. **Technical Support:** Degree of technical support provided to you by the customer, i.e., design feasibility, part functionality, etc.
2. **Technology Sharing:** Degree to which customer shares relevant technology with you.
3. **Quality Initiatives:** Communication of customer quality expectations and initiatives taken by the customer to help you achieve improved performance.
4. **Response to Cost Reduction Ideas:** Customer's responsiveness and openness to your cost reduction suggestions.
5. **Identification of Cost Drivers:** Customer's involvement in helping to identify major cost elements.
6. **Prints and Specifications:** Accuracy, ease of understanding, and applicability of customer's prints and specifications.
7. **Early Supplier Involvement:** Customer's willingness and ability to involve you early in the development process and incorporate your input into the design for better manufacturability.

B. Supplier Selection and Development:

8. **Purchasing Professionalism:** Manner in which customer's buyers represent themselves and their company.
9. **Professionalism in Conducting Supplier Surveys:** Regarding customer's evaluation of supplier's capability, performance and progress.
10. **Training/Education Effectiveness:** Content and usefulness of customer's formal supplier training programs.
11. **Commodity Management:** Effectiveness of customer's commodity management programs, if applicable to your company's products.
12. **Adherence to Policies/Procedures/Ethics:** Consistently high and uncompromising practice of customer's policies, procedures and integrity in business relationships.
13. **Negotiation and Award Process:** Process by which customer evaluates and awards business contracts.

C. Supplier Partnership:

14. **Partnership For Growth Process:** Formalized customer process to further the success of both the supplier and customer.
15. **Schedule Sharing:** Timeliness and ease of getting visibility to customer's production requirements.
16. **Schedule Quality:** Accuracy and variability of customer's scheduling information to you.
17. **Business Growth Potential:** Your potential for increased business from the customer.
18. **Improved Performance:** Improvement in your business performance resulting from relationship with customer.
19. **Communications and Feedback:** Customer's promptness and accuracy in providing information to you and listening to your suggestions and concerns.
20. **Preferred Status:** Realization of benefits resulting from Preferred Supplier status.
21. **Management Commitment to Partnership:** Commitment of customer's management to the partnership process.
22. **Purchasing Commitment to Partnership:** Commitment of customer's buyers to the partnership process.
23. **Engineering Commitment to Partnership:** Commitment of customer's engineers to the partnership process.
24. **Payment Terms:** Prompt payment in accordance with contractual agreements.

D. Summary:

25. **Overall Rating:** Current summary rating of customer.
26. **Recent Trend:** Customer's improvement trend during the last twelve months.
27. **Business Continuation:** Supplier's willingness to continue/expand business with customer.

AME Customer Survey

AME Customer Survey

ABOUT THE CUSTOMER RATING SURVEY

The following is intended to be a guide for you when writing your cover letter to the suppliers who will try out the form. We expect that most of you will tailor the letter to a specific supplier, and that you will add some items to the form that are of special interest to you.

This customer rating form is similar to one being used by a number of companies who want to improve their partnerships with suppliers.

The items, or "questions," appear lengthy, but they should not take long to complete. The extra verbiage is intended to help you select a response, and to prompt comments on how the customer can improve.

The (1)-to-(5) scale of responses to many items are written so that a (5) is an extremely demanding level of performance. Very few customers deserve a (5), so there's always room for improvement. It's expected that most companies eager to improve supplier partnerships today will score only a (2) or (3) on most items; sometimes a (4); and occasionally a (1). Since the purpose of this rating is to help the customer improve, please give an honest appraisal. Most welcome are specific suggestions for improvement -- even if the customer cannot adopt them quickly or easily.

To be of maximum value, this form should be completed by a person or team with across-the-board knowledge of your interaction with this customer.

Your comments or suggestions will be held in confidence by ------. Only aggregate data or responses to scaled items will be used in benchmark comparisons of this customer's performance with other companies. No specific names will be identified.

(This customer) and the Association for Manufacturing Excellence thank you for taking the time to complete this form. In addition, we thank you for participating with us to create better partnerships between customers and suppliers.

Customer Survey Form
(Association for Manufacturing Excellence, Jan. 1993)

Your Name & Company (optional) _____

You are asked to complete a survey on the performance as a customer of:

Customer company unit: Return it to:

_____   _____

_____   _____

Instructions: Please circle responses and add comments.

Coding of responses: For functions or activities shown:

1. Unacceptable   Prch. = Purchasing
2. Needs improvement   Acct. = Accounting
3. Meets expectation   Engr. = Engineering
4. Exceeds expectation   xxxx   = Cross out if inapplicable
5. Exceptional (best you have seen)   _____ = Write in

1. Do you trust the following contact points of this company?

Prch.   Acct.   Engr.   _____   _____   _____   _____
1 2 3 4 5   1 2 3 4 5   1 2 3 4 5   1 2 3 4 5   1 2 3 4 5   1 2 3 4 5   1 2 3 4 5

Comments:

2. Is communication in general clear and timely?

Prch.   Acct.   Engr.   _____   _____   _____   _____
1 2 3 4 5   1 2 3 4 5   1 2 3 4 5   1 2 3 4 5   1 2 3 4 5   1 2 3 4 5   1 2 3 4 5

Comments:

3. How well are quality expectations communicated?

Prch.   Acct.   Engr.   _____   _____   _____   _____
1 2 3 4 5   1 2 3 4 5   1 2 3 4 5   1 2 3 4 5   1 2 3 4 5   1 2 3 4 5   1 2 3 4 5

Comments:

4. How well does the company collaborate in continuous improvement?

Prch.   Acct.   Engr.   _____   _____   _____   _____
1 2 3 4 5   1 2 3 4 5   1 2 3 4 5   1 2 3 4 5   1 2 3 4 5   1 2 3 4 5   1 2 3 4 5

Comments:

AME Customer Survey

5. How well are agreed payment terms met?

Prch.   Acct.   Engr.   _____ _____ _____ _____
1 2 3 4 5   1 2 3 4 5   1 2 3 4 5   1 2 3 4 5   1 2 3 4 5   1 2 3 4 5   1 2 3 4 5

Comments:

6. How well do prices and terms reflect total costs to the customer, services provided, mutual improvement goals, and sharing of prosperity?

Prch.   Acct.   Engr.   _____ _____ _____ _____
1 2 3 4 5   1 2 3 4 5   1 2 3 4 5   1 2 3 4 5   1 2 3 4 5   1 2 3 4 5   1 2 3 4 5

Comments:

7. How well does the company collaborate on advanced product or process technology?

Prch.   Acct.   Engr.   _____ _____ _____ _____
1 2 3 4 5   1 2 3 4 5   1 2 3 4 5   1 2 3 4 5   1 2 3 4 5   1 2 3 4 5   1 2 3 4 5

Comments:

8. How does the company compare overall with all other customers?

Prch.   Acct.   Engr.   _____ _____ _____ _____
1 2 3 4 5   1 2 3 4 5   1 2 3 4 5   1 2 3 4 5   1 2 3 4 5   1 2 3 4 5   1 2 3 4 5

Comments:

9. Please comment on your overall experience with this customer in the past year or two. Are they improving? At what rate?

10. What one or two changes would you most like to see this customer make that would enable increased benefits to the two of you? In what areas would the greatest benefits be achieved (such as quality, cost, technical progress, dedicating of capacity to them, etc.)?

AME Meeting Evaluation

Association for Manufacturing Excellence
Meeting Evaluation Sheet

NAME: COMPANY:

DATE:

A. FOR EACH OF THE FOLLOWING AREAS, PLEASE INDICATE YOUR REACTION:

	EXCEEDED EXPECTATIONS	MET EXPECTATIONS	NEEDS IMPROVEMENT	NOT APPLICABLE
MEETING CONTENT				
Agenda was shown	☐	☐	☐	☐
Meeting was organized	☐	☐	☐	☐
Handout material supported the subject matter	☐	☐	☐	☐
Were the group activities effective	☐	☐	☐	☐
Were visual aids effective	☐	☐	☐	☐
Practicality of material discussed	☐	☐	☐	☐
Was the time spent on subject matter utilized properly	☐	☐	☐	☐
PRESENTERS				
Speaker responded well to questions	☐	☐	☐	☐
Covered the proper material clearly	☐	☐	☐	☐
Had knowledge of subject matter	☐	☐	☐	☐
Effective presentation style	☐	☐	☐	☐

B. YOUR SUGGESTIONS FOR IMPROVEMENT WOULD BE APPRECIATED:

_____

_____

_____

C. OTHER COMMENTS:

_____

_____

_____

PLEASE INDICATE THE RATING THAT BEST REFLECTS YOUR OVERALL EVALUATION OF THIS SESSION.

EXCELLENT	GOOD	FAIR	POOR
☐	☐	☐	☐

Partnership Diagnostic

Diagnose Your Partnership

Use the following diagnostic tool to help you evaluate the quality of any of your partnerships in the workplace. Answer the questions by checking Yes or No. Calculate your final score using the scheme at the bottom of the page. Studying your answers will give you insight into ways to improve the partnership.

1. We are compassionate coaches for each other.	Yes _ No _	11. We work independently without seeking each other's input. Yes _ No _
2. We acknowledge each other freely.	Yes _ No _	12 We forget to look at all the good work we have done together. We go on as if nothing special has happened. Yes _ No _
3. We are commited to a shared vision.	Yes _ No _	
4. We are able to generate and freely commit to strategic objectives based on our shared vision.	Yes _ No _	13. Our work together lacks direction and a cohesive design. Yes _ No _
		14. Our meetings together are tedious and without accomplishment. Yes _ No _
5. We value our accomplishments and display this pride by keeping accurate records of our achievements.	Yes _ No _	15. There seem to be hidden agendas and personal issues everywhere. Yes _ No _
6. Within the partnership, work is shared equally and without burden. We teach and learn from each other.	Yes _ No _	16. We isolate ourselves and others, working alone and with little or no support. If someone comes up with an idea, they own it. Yes _ No _
7. We constantly ask each other how we can do it better next time.	Yes _ No _	17. We have no idea how we handled a similar problem in the past. Yes _ No _
8. We speak in a way that is enrolling and enables everyone to be actively involved in a partnered undertaking.	Yes _ No _	18. When things go wrong, we easily blame each other or other groups. Yes _ No _
9. We share the benefits of our partnership with others outside the team.	Yes _ No _	19. The value that this partnership can give others is neglected. Yes _ No _
10. Our partnership is a model for others.	Yes _ No _	20. Our partnership benefits only ourselves. Yes _ No _

To find your partnership score, add the number of Yes answers in the left-hand column then subtract the number of Yes answers in the right-hand column. A score of +10 means you have a great partnership, +5 means most of the time it works, 0 means the partnership needs improvement to be viable, -5 means the partnership is not working , and -10 means the partnership is destructive. ◆

Index

About the Author

Patricia E. Moody is the president of Patricia E. Moody, Inc., a management consulting, training, and development firm that helps companies become better partners and make their operations faster and more flexible. She brings over twenty years' experience as a practitioner and a consultant—seven of which were with Rath and Strong of Lexington, Massachusetts—to a clients list that includes Digital Equipment Corporation, McNeil Consumer Laboratories, Fenwal, and Mead Corporation. She teaches operations management at Simmons College in Boston and conducts training and development workshops and seminars on partnering, manufacturing, and procurement productivity improvement. She has been an invited speaker at the Harvard Business School, the National Academy of Engineering, GE's Service Management Seminar, Babson College, and numerous APICS conferences. She is a coauthor of *Strategic Manufacturing* and author of features that have appeared in *Target* magazine, *Production and Inventory* magazine, *Business Horizons, Purchasing Insights*, and *Electronic Buyers News*. She is a certified member of the Institute of Management Consultants, editor of AME's *Target* magazine, and a member of AME's Northeast Board of Directors.